Starfish Café

Changing Lives One Recipe at a Time...

A partnership between Union Mission, Inc.
and Savannah Technical College

Starfish Café

Changing Lives One Recipe at a Time...

Published by Union Mission, Inc.

Student stories by Micheal Elliott
Original starfish painting by Sandy Branam
Photography by John Zeuli Photography, www.johnzeuliphotography.com

This cookbook is a collection of favorite recipes,
which are not necessarily original recipes.

ISBN: 978-0-9714243-1-9

Edited, Designed, and Manufactured by

CommunityClassics™

Favorite Recipes® Press
An imprint of

FRP™

P. O. Box 305142
Nashville, Tennessee 37230
(800) 358-0560
To obtain additional copies of *Starfish Café*,
use the order information at the back of this book or contact:
Union Mission, Inc.
120 Fahm Street
Savannah, Georgia 31401
(912) 236-7423
www.unionmission.org

All proceeds from *Starfish Café: Changing Lives One Recipe at a Time*
will benefit the operation of the Starfish Café.

Manufactured in China
First Printing: 2007
6,000 copies

The Today Show Visits the Starfish Café!

While Savannah has long known about the culinary delights awaiting them at the Café for breakfast and lunch, in 2005 it was discovered by the rest of the country! The Starfish Café was chosen for the *Today Show's* "Today Lends a Hand" segment, with Al Roker broadcasting live all morning from the Café! The viewing audience learned about the great food being served and the lives the Café is changing. After the show, the Union Mission Web site multiplied its normal hits, and people called from all over the country wanting to know how they could help! The Café was the proud recipient of many gifts from the show and its sponsors, including a Toyota van for catering events and multiple kitchen items to stock the kitchen. We were proud to host Al and the NBC family and want to thank them for letting everyone know what Savannah already knows: The Starfish Café is a great place to have a wonderful meal while also helping solve a social problem.

"We are proud of what you're doing here at the Starfish Café and thanks for taking care of the folks in Savannah!"

Al Roker, NBC *Today Show*

Foreword

Whenever someone visits the Starfish Café for the first time, they typically know that the restaurant is the home of a culinary arts training program for homeless and low-income people. They usually have heard that the Café has good food, and where else can you solve a social problem like poverty by merely having lunch? What draws the biggest surprise, though, is when the plate is brought to the waiting customer. First-timers and regulars alike stare in disbelief at a presentation that is in keeping with fine restaurants. Exclamations of praise are heard, and because homeless folks recall what it is like to go without, the portion sizes are huge!

Since the Café opened in 2001, customers have regularly asked-for recipes, be it our award-winning Bread-and-Butter Pudding or Poached Salmon with Lemon Butter Sauce and Sour Cream-Dill Potatoes, so it made sense to produce a cookbook. The recipes are often the result of negotiations between the chef instructors and the students who bring their own life experiences to building the menu. Many a new recipe begins when the student blurts out the question, "Why can't we add some of this?" It has led to some interesting culinary creations.

If the recipes weren't enough, this cookbook also provides us with the opportunity to celebrate some of our successes that go far beyond food. You will meet some of our graduates and learn of their incredible journeys through despair to triumph as they left poverty for careers creating culinary delights in kitchens throughout Savannah. While the food is good and the cookbook is fun, this is the real reason for the Starfish Café. I sincerely appreciate your support as we change lives, one culinary creation at a time.

Rev. Micheal Elliott,
President & CEO
Union Mission, Inc.
2007

Contents

A Special Word of Thanks
to Our Creative Contributors

Micheal Elliott is the President & CEO of Union Mission and has contributed the graduates' stories to the cookbook. Micheal is the author of eight books, including two novels, *Tour of Homes* and *Running With the Dolphins and Other Tybee Tales*, and works of nonfiction, including the award-winning *Why The Homeless Don't Have Homes and What to Do About It* and *Playing Hide and Seek: A Non-Churchgoer's Path to Finding God*. Micheal's professional work has been recognized nationally by the American Hospital Association, the Robert Wood Johnson Foundation, and the U. S. Department of Housing and Urban Development. He is a popular speaker and lives with his wife, Julie, and their dog, Goddess, on Tybee Island, Georgia.

Sandy Branam has been a storyteller all of her life. She has been a professional artist since 1998, experimenting "as the situation calls for it" in sculpture, drawing, and painting. A former Montessori school teacher, Sandy loves capturing people who are doing things, especially using their hands to work. This regard for people at work draws her repeatedly to the Starfish Café. Sandy thinks it's "the best thing I've heard of for people who have problems and want to turn their life around." Sandy's painting on the cover of the cookbook was inspired by the "starfish story" adapted from an essay in *The Star Thrower* by Loren Eiseley, about a man witnessing someone throwing starfish back into the ocean; when he asks why he would attempt to throw them back when there are so many, the response is that at least one has been saved! Sandy was also inspired by the locally well-known character, Arthur, and by the north end of Tybee Island, Georgia.

To contact Sandy, call (912) 308-8286
or email her: savbranart@bellsouth.net.

6

People are the heart and common denominator of John Zeuli's photography. John believes good portrait photography touches the subject's essence. It reflects the Spirit within the person. This, in turn, touches the viewer. The observer might not be able to explain how or why, yet the viewer is drawn to the photograph, perhaps even pulled in. Good photography is about Spirit touching Spirit. To this end, his photography is vibrant, compelling, and authentic in the sense that it feels "real." It is not static. Even formal photographs can, and should, reflect life and a sense of immediacy. During the past twenty years, John's photography has encompassed Olympic Gold Medalists, film stars, authors, families, and individuals. His portrait exhibits have been commissioned by major institutions and shown throughout the country, including the United States Senate and the United Nations. More of John's work may be seen at www.johnzeuliphotography.com.

Acknowledgments

This effort was largely accomplished through the efforts of
Chef Rachel Petraglia and Julie Walsh-Elliott, however such an
undertaking is never the result of just a couple of individuals.

Chef Lotinza Clark, Ailerua Crawford, Laura Webb, Rebekah Gonzalez,
Chef Gloria Clements, and the entire Union Mission staff
contributed to making this cookbook a reality.

Dr. C. B. Rathburn and the staff of Savannah Technical College
regularly contribute their experience and expertise to our efforts.

The Board of Directors of Union Mission provides oversight
and guidance to the Café on an ongoing basis.

Former Board Member Ben S. Barnes and his wife, Bettye, regularly offer tips to
improve how we do things and help us be better at what we do.

Finally, it is the students themselves who deserve the real credit. They are the
ones who prove on a daily basis that the human spirit can accomplish anything
that it wishes once it becomes determined. This book is dedicated to them.

*When the culinary arts program was established, it was blessed to have instructor
Chef Michael Wilson (left) assigned from Savannah Technical College.
As the program evolved, Chef Mike moved the program into a freestanding restaurant—
The Starfish Café. Since then, the Café has benefited from other caring
instructors—Chef Shelley Rubitsky, Chef Robert Hanne' (right), Chef Gloria Clements,
and Chef Lotinza Clark. For the past four years, Chef Rachel Petraglia (middle)
has overseen the Café and the education of the students.*

History of the Partners of the Starfish Café Collaboration

UNION MISSION, INC.

Union Mission, Inc. exists to end and prevent homelessness in the greater region of Savannah, Georgia. A nonprofit 501-©-3 corporation, Union Mission is an outcome performance-based organization that has quantified results of ending homelessness for more than two thousand people over the past ten years. A result such as this is accomplished through a series of diverse and innovative programs, each attacking a causal factor of homelessness. Union Mission has been recognized as a best practice by the U.S. Department of Housing and Urban Development, the Georgia Department of Community Affairs, the American Hospital Association, the Georgia Hospital Association, and the Robert Wood Johnson Foundation. Union Mission's programs have been profiled by CNN, the *Today Show* and *USA Today*. Learn more about Union Mission at www.unionmission.org or www.thestarfishcafe.org.

SAVANNAH TECHNICAL COLLEGE

At Savannah Technical College, we believe in creating opportunities for people to improve their lives through technical education. When you enroll at Savannah Technical College, you'll be able to choose from more than fifty different careers in fields ranging from nursing to computer networking, from culinary arts to automotive repair, and everything in between. And it only takes a short investment of your time.

Our certificate programs can be completed in just a quarter or two and can prepare you to start in a new career or help you get that promotion you're looking for with your current employer. Our diploma programs take about a year to complete, and our associate degree programs can be completed in about two years. Many of the degree programs transition directly to area universities, creating even greater opportunities for our students! Stop by the campus nearest you or visit us on the Web at www.savannahtech.edu. You'll find an opportunity waiting just for you.

9

A Historical Look at the Starfish Café

On April 17, 2000, with only six students and using a kitchen in a homeless shelter, the Culinary Arts Program was established. The program was a collaborative effort involving the Employment & Training Center of Union Mission, Inc., America's Second Harvest of Coastal Georgia, and Savannah Technical College targeting homeless and low-income individuals. At the end of the first class, most of the graduates were successful in getting jobs! The partners looked at each other and agreed to continue doing it.

After several classes, and numerous job placements, it was decided that a restaurant should be established to showcase the students and their food. In 2001, the Culinary Arts Program opened the doors of the Bread & Butter Café to serve the public. In 2004, the collaborative partnership underwent restructuring, and as a result the café was renamed the Starfish Café, with Union Mission and Savannah Technical College as collaborative partners.

The program curriculum consists of three major components: Culinary Arts training, Life Skills/Work Readiness classes, and work experience in the Starfish Café. Students receive instruction in the fundamentals of cooking, food safety, sanitation procedures, nutrition, and French culinary techniques. Students graduate with a Certificate in Culinary Arts from Savannah Technical College, which is often the first time many have ever accomplished such a feat.

Years later, the students continue to graduate and obtain jobs in the food service industry. Some have even gone on to open their own food service businesses! All this while ending their homelessness! The success continues…

10

The Starfish Gala

Black ties. Evening gowns. The smooth stylings of Savannah jazz legend Ben Tucker. Overlooking the Savannah River from the candlelit Scarbrough Ballroom at the Hyatt Regency. Exquisite food by Savannah's finest culinary minds. Silent and live auctions for a very good cause. A celebration of the redeeming power of hard work, determination, and experience. The Starfish Gala!

The Gala began in April 2006 as the official annual "black-tie event" and has quickly evolved into one of Savannah's come-heck-or-high-water, must-attend spring events. The evening allows our patrons and benefactors to have their taste buds tickled and treated by local chefs' unique food-and-wine pairings. In 2006, a dozen of Savannah's finest restaurants participated: The Hyatt Regency, George's, 514 West, Garibaldi's, Vic's on the River, The Cobblestone Conch House, Cha Bella, Nick Mueller's Catering, The Pink House, The Pirates' House, Bazil's, and Mug Shots.

A pair of guest speakers—two graduates of the program—spoke from the heart about the dramatic life changes that the Starfish Café helped bring about in their lives. There was not a dry eye in the room.

Each year the event raises funds to help continue the mission of the Starfish Café in the Savannah community as well as spreads awareness of the work being done and the lives being transformed by the Culinary Arts Program.

To reserve your seat or learn more about how you can get involved, please visit our Web site at www.thestarfishcafe.org, or just come by the Café.

Breakfast

Best-Ever Pancakes

Fruity Ten-Grain Pancakes

Plantain Pancakes with Spiced Rum Maple Syrup

Baked Pecan French Toast

Breakfast Casserole

Smoked Salmon and Eggs Benedict

Garden Frittata

Breakfast BLT Sandwiches

Maple-Apple Sausage Patties

Raspberry Coffee Cake

Lemon Poppy Seed Bread

Apple Streusel Muffins

Carrot and Zucchini Muffins

Chocolate Zucchini Muffins

Blueberry Lemon Scones

Homemade Granola

Trail Mix

Fruit Smoothie

Breakfast Starts at the Café

Juane Kent

Standing on the corner with other kids who may or may not be his friends had Juane wondering what he was going to do with his future. The kids hanging out with him simply seemed to be interested in just that…hanging out. Then one day he saw a flyer recruiting anyone interested in a culinary arts training program at the Starfish Café. It went on to say that he could graduate with a certificate from Savannah Technical College; that sounded better than hanging out, so Juane enrolled in the program.

"I came to the café because I love to cook," he explains. "I wanted the opportunity to better my education so that I can pursue my career. I was looking out for myself."

During his time in the program, he found who he was looking for. He changed his group of friends to other students who loved cooking and others who already had jobs in the restaurant industry. When asked about the people that he used to hang with, the normally soft-spoken and mild-mannered Juane is emphatic, "I don't want nothing to do with them. They can't help me!"

Upon graduation, he was immediately employed by the Cobblestone Conch House where he has been for the past two years.

"This has been great, but I want to go further and own my own restaurant. My special will be spaghetti!"

Pam Culver

Pam sat under the tree drinking beer. The tree is a gathering place for those who spend their days drinking and their nights passed out under the stars. "The tree will hinder you," she explains. "When you're under the tree you forget about doctor's appointments. You forget to go get your food stamps. You forget reality under the tree."

As she drank her beer, she saw one of her friends dressed in a white coat walking on the other side of the street. He had often sat under the tree with her.

"What's up?" she yelled over to him.

"I'm in school," he answered with a smile on his face.

"Where?"

"The Starfish Café!" came the reply as he kept walking.

Pam couldn't get the thought of going back to school out of her mind. "Oh boy, I was a troubled person. I was homeless. I stayed on the streets. I had a drug and alcohol addiction. I had been in and out of jail. It seemed that this was my only purpose. I was afraid of change, so I stayed under the tree."

A month later, Pam found the courage to try. She enrolled in the culinary arts program and passed the entrance test. Then she heard the instructor say that all students would be required to submit to random drug tests while in the class. Pam immediately got up and left the classroom and walked to a drug store to find something to alter the results of a drug test. Returning to the class, she lasted twelve weeks before she relapsed.

She returned to the tree. Then she returned to jail. Then while on probation, she was required to get a job. Working part-time as a server at the Savannah International Trade and Convention Center, Pam felt good wearing the white coat and black pants and remembered the Starfish Café. She enrolled again.

"It was the proudest day of my life because they gave me the drug test and I passed. I was so proud that I hugged the lady who gave it to me, and then I asked her for a copy of the results so that I could show the world!"

Pam was determined this time. She vowed to finish what she was starting. She knew that she had to graduate or die. In addition to a full day in the culinary arts training program, Pam was also attending group treatment for substance abuse and having to report weekly to drug court.

"It taught me how to get organized," she explains. "I started writing things down, keeping a calendar, and then things started getting smoother."

The more time passed, the more time she found was hers.

Upon graduation, Pam enrolled at Savannah Technical College for additional culinary arts education. She worked two jobs. One was as a cook for a social club serving as many as fifty guests at a time. The other was at a convenience store.

"Now I live for my recovery and attend an Alcoholics Anonymous meeting every day. I'm still looking to get better," she says, "and my next job will be Monday through Friday. I can't wait!"

Best-Ever Pancakes

1 cup plus 2 tablespoons all-purpose flour
3 tablespoons sugar
1 1/2 teaspoons baking powder
1/2 teaspoon salt
Grated zest of 4 lemons
3/4 cup whole milk ricotta cheese
6 tablespoons milk
6 tablespoons unsalted butter, melted
3 egg yolks, lightly beaten
2 tablespoons fresh lemon juice
1 teaspoon vanilla extract
3 egg whites
1 cup fresh blueberries
Unsalted butter for cooking

Mix the flour, sugar, baking powder, salt and lemon zest in a bowl. Combine the ricotta cheese, milk, 6 tablespoons butter, the egg yolks, lemon juice and vanilla in a bowl and mix well. Add the ricotta cheese mixture to the flour mixture and whisk until combined. Beat the egg whites in a mixing bowl until soft peaks form. Fold the egg whites into the batter and gently stir in the blueberries.

Melt additional unsalted butter in a large skillet over medium heat. Pour 1/4 cup or the desired amount of the batter for each pancake into the hot skillet, allowing approximately 2 to 3 inches between each pancake. Cook until bubbles appear on the surface and the underside is golden brown. Turn and cook for 2 to 3 minutes longer or until golden brown on the remaining side. Remove the pancakes to a baking sheet and keep warm in a 200-degree oven. Serve warm with maple syrup.
Serves 4

Warm maple syrup before drizzling on the pancakes. For extra-special occasions, heat the syrup with 1/2 cup raspberries until the berries plump and burst.

Photograph for this recipe is shown on page 13.

Fruity Ten-Grain Pancakes

1 cup ten-grain pancake mix
1/2 cup sour cream
1 egg, lightly beaten
1 tablespoon honey
1 teaspoon vanilla extract

Milk
1/2 cup blueberries
1/2 cup sliced banana
1/2 cup sliced strawberries
Canola oil for cooking

Combine the first five ingredients in a bowl and mix well. Blend in enough milk
to reach a smooth consistency, stirring constantly. Fold in the fruit.

    Heat a small amount of canola oil in a large skillet over medium heat. Pour 1/4 cup
of the batter for each pancake into the hot skillet, leaving 2 to 3 inches between
each pancake. Cook until bubbles appear on the surface and the underside is golden
brown. Turn and cook until golden brown on the remaining side. Remove to a heated
platter or keep warm in a 200-degree oven. Serve with butter and maple syrup.
Serves 6

Ten-grain pancake mix is available at most health food stores.

Plantain Pancakes with Spiced Rum Maple Syrup

Pancakes
1 cup all-purpose flour
1 tablespoon baking powder
2 teaspoons brown sugar
1 teaspoon salt
1 cup plus 2 tablespoons milk
1 cup finely chopped ripe plantain

1 egg, lightly beaten
Unsalted butter for cooking

Spiced Rum Maple Syrup
2 cups maple syrup
3 tablespoons spiced rum

To prepare the pancakes, mix the flour, baking powder, brown sugar and salt
in a bowl. Whisk in the milk, plantain and egg until combined. Melt a small amount
of butter on a griddle or in a large sauté pan over medium-high heat. Pour 1/4 cup
or the desired amount of batter for each pancake onto the hot griddle, leaving 2 to
3 inches between each pancake. Cook until bubbles appear on the surface and the
underside is golden brown. Turn the pancakes and cook for 2 minutes longer. Remove
to a heated platter or keep warm in a 200-degree oven.

To prepare the syrup, mix the syrup and spiced rum in a microwave-safe bowl.
Microwave for 1 minute or until heated through. Serve with the pancakes.
Serves 4 to 6

Bananas may be substituted for the plantains.

Baked Pecan French Toast

1 cup packed brown sugar
$1/2$ cup (1 stick) unsalted butter, softened
2 tablespoons honey
1 cup chopped pecans, toasted
1 (1-pound) loaf sliced Texas toast
16 ounces cream cheese, cubed and softened
$12/3$ cups milk
6 eggs, beaten
1 tablespoon granulated sugar
1 teaspoon vanilla extract
$1/2$ teaspoon ground cinnamon
$1/4$ teaspoon ground ginger
$1/8$ teaspoon ground nutmeg
$1/8$ teaspoon ground cloves

Combine the brown sugar, butter and honey in a 1-quart saucepan. Cook over medium heat for 2 to 3 minutes or until blended, stirring frequently. Pour the brown sugar mixture into a 9×13-inch baking dish that has been sprayed with nonstick cooking spray, tilting the dish to ensure even coverage. Layer with the pecans, half the bread slices and the cream cheese.

Combine the milk, eggs, granulated sugar, vanilla, cinnamon, ginger, nutmeg and cloves in a mixing bowl and beat until blended. Dip one side of each of the remaining bread slices in the egg mixture and arrange the slices coated side down over the cream cheese. Gradually pour the remaining egg mixture over the prepared layers. Chill, covered, for 4 to 10 hours; remove the cover.

Bake at 350 degrees for 50 to 55 minutes or until the top is golden brown and a knife inserted in the center comes out clean. Let stand for 10 minutes and cut into eight equal portions. Invert each serving onto a plate and serve with maple syrup if desired.
Serves 8

Breakfast Casserole

1 pound bulk pork sausage
1 pound bacon, crisp-cooked and crumbled
10 slices white sandwich bread, cubed
2 cups (8 ounces) shredded sharp Cheddar cheese
1 cup instant grits, cooked
2 cups milk
6 eggs
1 teaspoon salt
1 teaspoon pepper

Brown the sausage in a skillet, stirring until crumbly; drain. Toss the sausage, bacon, bread cubes and cheese in a bowl. Add the grits and stir until combined.

Whisk the milk, eggs, salt and pepper in a bowl until blended. Stir into the grits mixture. Spoon the grits mixture into a lightly greased 9×13-inch baking dish and bake at 350 degrees for 45 minutes or until set. Let stand for 5 minutes before serving.
Serves 8

You may prepare the casserole one day in advance and store, covered, in the refrigerator. Bake as directed above. For variety, add sautéed onions, sautéed mushrooms, and sautéed bell peppers to the sausage mixture.

Smoked Salmon and Eggs Benedict

Hollandaise Sauce
1/2 cup white wine vinegar
2 tablespoons water
4 egg yolks, lightly beaten
1 cup clarified butter, heated
2 teaspoons chopped fresh dill weed
1/2 teaspoon fresh lemon juice
Salt and freshly ground white pepper
    to taste

Eggs Benedict
4 English muffins, split
3 tablespoons unsalted butter
8 eggs
8 slices smoked salmon
4 slices red onion
4 slices red tomato
2 tablespoons capers

To prepare the sauce, bring the vinegar and water to a boil in a small saucepan. Reduce the heat to low and simmer for 3 minutes to allow the mixture to reduce. Remove from the heat and cool slightly. Whisk in the eggs yolks until combined and pour into a heatproof bowl. Place the bowl over but not touching simmering water in a small saucepan over low heat. Cook for 3 to 4 minutes or until thickened and pale yellow in color, whisking constantly. Process the egg yolk mixture in a blender until smooth. Let cool for 1 minute. Add the clarified butter gradually, processing constantly until the butter is incorporated. Add the dill weed and lemon juice and process until combined. Season with salt and white pepper. Pour the sauce into a double boiler and keep warm over very low heat. For a quick-and-easy version of this sauce, purchase packets of Hollandaise sauce at your local supermarket.

To prepare the eggs Benedict, spread the cut side of each muffin with approximately 1 teaspoon of the butter. Arrange the muffins butter side up on a baking sheet and broil for 3 to 5 minutes or until golden brown. Turn off the broiler and cover the muffins with foil. Keep warm in the oven.

Add enough water to an egg-poacher to measure 1/2 inch. Bring to a simmer over medium heat. Lightly coat the poaching cups with nonstick cooking spray. Crack one egg into each cup. Cover and cook for 3 minutes or until the whites are firm and the yolks are glazed over but still soft, or to the desired degree of doneness. Remove the eggs to a heated platter.

To serve, place two muffin halves on each of four serving plates. Layer each serving with 2 slices of the salmon, 1 slice of the onion and 1 slice of the tomato. Sprinkle evenly with the capers. Top each serving with two poached eggs and drizzle with the sauce. Serve immediately.
Serves 4

To clarify butter, heat 1 cup of unsalted butter in a saucepan over medium heat until completely melted; do not stir. Turn off the heat. Using a ladle, gently skim the top to remove all the white milk solids that have risen to the top. Pour the clarified butter into a small pitcher, being careful not to pour in the milk solids that have dropped to the bottom of the saucepan.

Garden Frittata

2 tablespoons olive oil
1/4 cup finely chopped zucchini
1/4 cup finely chopped yellow onion
1/4 cup finely chopped mushrooms
1/4 cup finely chopped red bell pepper
6 eggs
1/4 cup milk
1 tablespoon minced fresh flat-leaf parsley
Salt and freshly ground pepper to taste
2/3 cup shredded smoked Gouda cheese
2 tablespoons unsalted butter

Heat the olive oil in a medium sauté pan. Add the zucchini, onion, mushrooms and bell pepper to the hot oil and cook for 3 to 4 minutes or until light brown and tender. Let stand until cool. Whisk the eggs, milk, parsley, salt and pepper in a bowl until combined. Stir in the cheese and zucchini mixture.

Melt the butter in a large deep nonstick sauté pan over medium heat. Add the egg mixture to the hot butter, tilting the pan to ensure even coverage. Cook for 5 to 6 minutes, gently lifting the edge of the frittata occasionally with a rubber spatula to allow the uncooked egg mixture to flow underneath. Flip the frittata and cook for 3 to 5 minutes longer or until the frittata is cooked through and golden brown. Loosen the edge with a rubber spatula and gently slide onto a plate. Cut into wedges and serve warm or at room temperature.

Serves 4

For variety, sprinkle the warm frittata wedges with chopped red tomato. The cool tomato tastes great with the warm frittata and the bright red adds a colorful and easy garnish.

21

Breakfast BLT Sandwiches

8 eggs, lightly beaten
1/4 cup milk
Salt and pepper to taste
8 slices sourdough bread, toasted

8 slices red tomato
8 leaves leaf lettuce
8 slices maple bacon, crisp-cooked
   and drained

Whisk the eggs, milk, salt and pepper in a bowl until blended. Scramble the egg mixture in a medium sauté pan to the desired degree of doneness. Remove from the heat and cover to keep warm.

    Assemble each sandwich with 2 slices of the bread, 2 slices of the tomato, 2 lettuce leaves, 2 slices of the bacon and one-fourth of the scrambled eggs. Dress to your liking with mayonnaise or butter.

Makes 4 sandwiches

Maple-Apple Sausage Patties

1 tablespoon canola oil
1/2 yellow onion, minced
1 pound mild pork sausage
1 Granny Smith apple, peeled and
   finely chopped

2 tablespoons maple syrup
1 tablespoon minced fresh sage
Salt and pepper to taste

Heat the canola oil in a small sauté pan over medium heat and add the onion. Sauté for 5 to 6 minutes or until tender. Remove the onion to a bowl using a slotted spoon, reserving the pan drippings.

    Combine the sausage, apple, syrup, sage, sautéed onion, salt and pepper in a bowl and mix well. Divide the sausage mixture into twelve equal portions and shape each portion into a patty. Cook the patties in the reserved pan drippings until cooked through and brown; drain.

Makes 1 dozen sausage patties

Raspberry Coffee Cake

Streusel
3/4 cup all-purpose flour
1/3 cup packed light brown sugar
1/4 cup granulated sugar
1 teaspoon ground cinnamon
Pinch of ground cloves
6 tablespoons unsalted butter, chilled
    and cut into small pieces

Coffee Cake
1 1/2 cups all-purpose flour
3/4 cup sugar

2 teaspoons baking powder
1/2 teaspoon salt
1/2 cup milk
1/4 cup (1/2 stick) unsalted
    butter, melted
1 egg
1 1/2 teaspoons vanilla extract
1 teaspoon almond extract
2 cups fresh raspberries

To prepare the streusel, mix the flour, brown sugar, granulated sugar, cinnamon and cloves in a bowl. Cut the butter into the flour mixture using a pastry blender or fork until coarse crumbs form.

To prepare the coffee cake, mix the flour, sugar, baking powder and salt in a bowl. Combine the milk, butter, egg and flavorings in a mixing bowl and beat at medium speed for 1 minute or until creamy. Add the creamed mixture to the flour mixture and mix until combined.

Spoon the batter into a greased and floured 9-inch springform pan. Sprinkle with the raspberries and gently press the berries into the batter. Top with the streusel and bake at 350 degrees for 40 to 45 minutes or until a wooden pick inserted in the center comes out clean. Cool in the pan on a wire rack for 20 minutes. Remove the side of the pan and cut the coffee cake into wedges to serve.

Makes 1 (9-inch) coffee cake

You may substitute an equal amount of any fresh fruit for the raspberries.

Lemon Poppy Seed Bread

1 1/2 cups all-purpose flour
2 tablespoons poppy seeds
1/2 teaspoon baking powder
1/4 teaspoon baking soda
1/4 teaspoon salt
3/4 cup sugar
2/3 cup unsalted butter, softened
1/3 cup lemon yogurt
2 eggs
1 tablespoon freshly grated lemon zest
1 teaspoon vanilla extract
1/2 cup milk

Combine the flour, poppy seeds, baking powder, baking soda and salt in a bowl and mix well. Beat the sugar and butter in a large mixing bowl at medium speed until creamy, scraping the bowl frequently. Add the yogurt, eggs, lemon zest and vanilla to the creamed mixture and mix well. Reduce the speed to low and alternately add the flour mixture and milk, beating just until moistened after each addition.

Spoon the batter into a 4×8-inch loaf pan sprayed with nonstick cooking spray. Bake at 350 degrees for 55 to 60 minutes or until a wooden pick inserted in the center comes out clean. Cool in the pan for 10 minutes. Remove to a wire rack to cool completely.

Makes 1 (4×8-inch) loaf

Apple Streusel Muffins

Streusel
3/4 cup all-purpose flour
1/3 cup packed light brown sugar
1/4 cup granulated sugar
1 teaspoon ground cinnamon
Pinch of ground cloves
6 tablespoons unsalted butter, chilled
    and cut into small pieces

Muffins
1 1/2 cups all-purpose flour
3/4 cup sugar
1 1/2 teaspoons baking powder
1 teaspoon ground cinnamon
1/2 cup milk
1/3 cup butter, melted
1 egg, lightly beaten
1 cup finely chopped apple

To prepare the streusel, mix the flour, brown sugar, granulated sugar, cinnamon and cloves in a bowl. Cut the butter into the flour mixture using a pastry blender or fork until coarse crumbs form.

To prepare the muffins, combine the flour, sugar, baking powder and cinnamon in a medium bowl and mix well. Mix the milk, butter, egg and apple in a bowl. Stir the apple mixture into the flour mixture just until moistened.

Spoon the batter into twelve greased muffin cups. Sprinkle the streusel over the tops and gently press it into the batter. Bake at 375 degrees for 18 to 23 minutes or until light brown. Cool in the pan for 5 minutes. Serve warm with butter and/or jam.
Makes 1 dozen muffins

Carrot and Zucchini Muffins

1 cup all-purpose flour
1 cup whole wheat flour
1/2 cup sugar
1 teaspoon baking powder
1 teaspoon ground cinnamon
1/2 teaspoon baking soda

1/2 teaspoon salt
3/4 cup orange juice
1/2 cup canola oil
1 egg, lightly beaten
1 cup grated carrots (about 2 carrots)
1 cup grated zucchini (about 1 zucchini)

Mix the all-purpose flour, whole wheat flour, sugar, baking powder, cinnamon, baking soda and salt in a bowl. Whisk the orange juice, canola oil and egg in a bowl until blended. Add the flour mixture and mix just until moistened. Fold in the carrots and zucchini.

Spoon the batter into twelve greased muffin cups. Bake at 375 degrees for 25 to 30 minutes or until the muffins test done. Cool in the pan for 5 minutes.

Makes 1 dozen muffins

Chocolate Zucchini Muffins

3 cups all-purpose flour
1 1/2 teaspoons baking powder
1 teaspoon baking soda
1 teaspoon salt
3 cups sugar
1 1/2 cups vegetable oil
4 eggs

3 ounces unsweetened baking
  chocolate, melted
3 cups grated zucchini
  (about 3 zucchini)
1 cup walnuts, chopped
1 cup (6 ounces) chocolate chips

Sift the flour, baking powder, baking soda and salt together. Combine the sugar, oil and eggs in a mixing bowl and beat at medium speed until combined. Reduce the speed to low and add the flour mixture, beating constantly just until moistened. Add the chocolate and mix well. Fold in the zucchini, walnuts and chocolate chips.

Spoon the batter into twelve greased muffin cups. Bake at 350 degrees for 20 to 25 minutes or until a wooden pick inserted in the centers comes out clean. Cool in the pan for 5 minutes. Remove to a wire rack to cool completely.

Makes 1 dozen muffins

Blueberry Lemon Scones

Scones
13/4 cups all-purpose flour
1 cup fresh blueberries
1/4 cup sugar
1 tablespoon freshly grated lemon zest
11/2 teaspoons baking powder
1/2 teaspoon baking soda
1/4 teaspoon salt
1/4 cup (1/2 stick) unsalted butter, chilled
1/4 cup sour cream
1 egg, lightly beaten
3 tablespoons lemon juice
1 teaspoon almond flavoring

Confectioners' Sugar Glaze
1/2 cup confectioners' sugar
1 teaspoon unsalted butter, softened
1/8 teaspoon almond flavoring
2 to 3 teaspoons milk

To prepare the scones, mix the flour, blueberries, sugar, lemon zest, baking powder, baking soda and salt in a large bowl. Cut in the butter with a pastry blender or fork until coarse crumbs form. Combine the sour cream, egg, lemon juice and flavoring in a small bowl and mix well. Add the sour cream mixture to the blueberry mixture and stir for 1 minute or just until moistened.

Knead the dough on a lightly floured surface five to eight times or until smooth. Pat into a 7-inch round on a greased baking sheet. Score into six wedges; do not separate. Bake at 375 degrees for 18 to 25 minutes or until light brown. Cool on the baking sheet for 10 minutes. Remove to a platter and cut into six wedges.

To prepare the glaze, mix the confectioners' sugar, butter, flavoring and desired amount of milk in a bowl until of a glaze consistency. Drizzle the glaze over the warm scones.
Makes 6 scones

Homemade Granola

2 cups old-fashioned oats
1/2 cup wheat germ
1/4 cup coarsely chopped walnuts
1/4 cup sliced almonds
1/4 cup shredded sweetened coconut
3 tablespoons honey
2 tablespoons canola oil
1 teaspoon ground cinnamon
1/4 cup dried cranberries
1/4 cup golden raisins

Combine the oats, wheat germ, walnuts, almonds and coconut in a bowl and mix well. Spread in a single layer on a large rimmed baking sheet and place the baking sheet on the lowest oven rack. Broil with the oven door slightly ajar for 2 to 3 minutes or until crisp and golden brown, shaking the baking sheet every 30 seconds while keeping the mixture in an even layer. Watch the mixture carefully so it does not burn. Remove the oats mixture to a large plate to cool and then pour into a large bowl.

Combine the honey, canola oil and cinnamon in a small saucepan and mix well. Cook over low heat for 2 minutes or until heated through, stirring occasionally. Add half the honey mixture to the oats mixture and toss to combine. Add just enough of the remaining honey mixture so that the granola clumps slightly but is not soupy. Stir in the cranberries and raisins. Serve with yogurt and sliced fresh fruit.
Serves 4

Trail Mix

1 cup (6 ounces) semisweet
   chocolate chips
1/2 cup walnut halves
1/4 cup butterscotch chips
1/4 cup dried cherries

1/4 cup golden raisins
1/4 cup dried apricots, chopped
1/4 cup dried apples, chopped
1/4 cup cashews
1/4 cup pistachios

Mix the chocolate chips, walnuts, butterscotch chips, cherries, raisins, apricots, apples, cashews and pistachios in a medium bowl. Store in an airtight container.
Makes about 3 1/4 cups

Fruit Smoothie

1 1/2 cups plain yogurt
1 cup ice
1 banana, sliced
1 cup strawberries, cut into halves
1 cup sliced peeled fresh peach

1/4 cup blueberries
1/4 cup orange juice
Grated zest and juice of 1 lime
1 teaspoon minced fresh mint

Combine the yogurt, ice, banana, strawberries, peach, blueberries, orange juice, lime zest, lime juice and mint in a blender. Process until smooth and serve immediately.
Serves 4

29

Lunch

Antipasto Salad

Curry Chicken Salad

Grilled Cajun Chicken Salad

Thai Chicken Salad

Chicken and Wild Rice Salad

Pesto Chicken Salad

Tuna Salad

Shrimp and Avocado Caesar Salad

Bean Salad

Black-Eyed Pea Salad

Creamy Cucumber Salad

Cucumber and Tomato Salad

Blue Cheese, Green Apple
and Pecan Salad

Fruit and Honey Spinach Salad

Coleslaw

Pesto Pizza

White Pizza

Philly Cheesesteak Sandwiches

Roast Beef and Blue Cheese Sandwiches

Spicy Roast Beef Subs with
Tomato Garlic Sauce

Meatball Sandwiches

Maple Bacon, Tomato and Avocado
Cheese Sandwiches

Muffuletta

Italian Club Sandwiches

Salami, Provolone and Ham Sandwiches
with Caper Relish

Club Sandwiches with Olive Cream Cheese

Smoked Turkey, Bacon and
Grilled Apple Wraps

Turkey Sausage Sandwiches

Grilled Mexican Chicken Sandwiches

Chicken Teriyaki Sandwiches

Shrimp Po' Boys with Rémoulade Sauce

Tarragon-Egg Salad Sandwiches

Eggplant Parmesan Sandwiches

Cheese-Stuffed Portobello
Mushroom Sandwiches

Tomato, Basil and Mozzarella Sandwiches

Lunchtime at the Café

Portia Quaintance

Portia loves her church and is excited to be counted as one of its ministers, helping the pastor serve wherever he needs her. She was doing housework and living on 41st Street as she helped with the church's ministries. Then one day she received a flyer in the mail recruiting students for the culinary arts training program at the Starfish Café. Because she loved to cook and suspected that it might help her ability to give more to the church, she enrolled.

At first she was excited, but there were several students who had a difficult time working as a team. Many days, they would lapse into bickering with one another instead of assisting each other to complete assigned tasks. One of the aspects of the program is a Life Skills Curriculum that focuses on team building and conflict resolution. Portia found the tools that she needed to work through the difficult work environment.

One day the Café hosted a book signing with two authors—Georgia Department of Labor Commissioner Michael Thurmond and Union Mission President & CEO Micheal Elliott. Portia was part of the student staff that Saturday morning. Both authors read from their books and answered questions from the audience. Portia was captivated.

"That day I learned that if those authors can accomplish something like writing books while they were busy doing other things, then I can accomplish what I want. It was such an inspiration to me that I went on to complete the program."

"Graduation was the happiest day of my life," she tearfully says now, "because I finally completed something."

After graduation, her church asked her to relocate to Florida to support a mission effort. Portia soon opened her own restaurant, serving soul food to hungry customers, including many parishioners.

Two years later, she was asked to return to Savannah and serve the home church again. Soon she was the victim of identity theft, which forced her into homelessness. Now she is relying on her faith and has returned to the Starfish Café until she can recover.

Portia smiles broadly as she tells her story signifying her deep faith. "My passion is making people happy and making them good food! I can do that through my cooking. And that makes me happy!"

Regardless of the difficulty that she may find herself in, Portia relies on her faith and her ability to cook to get her through.

"The Café is all about bettering me," she says. "This is my home and it makes me feel good inside."

Antipasto Salad

1/4 cup red wine vinegar
1 teaspoon dried oregano
1/2 teaspoon dried basil
1/2 teaspoon parsley flakes
1/2 cup olive oil
Salt and pepper to taste
4 cups mixed salad greens
4 (1/2-inch) slices Genoa
    salami, chopped

4 (1/2-inch) slices provolone
    cheese, chopped
4 (1/2-inch) slices pepperoni, chopped
1 green bell pepper, chopped
2 ribs celery, chopped
1 purple onion, chopped
1 cup cherry tomatoes, cut into halves
4 hard-cooked eggs, cut into quarters
8 pepperoncini chiles

Whisk the vinegar, oregano, basil and parsley in a bowl until combined. Add the olive oil gradually, whisking constantly until the oil is incorporated. Season with salt and pepper.

Mix the salad greens, salami, cheese, pepperoni, bell pepper, celery, onion and tomatoes in a large bowl. Add the vinaigrette and toss to coat. Arrange the salad evenly on serving plates or in a serving bowl. Top with the eggs and pepperoncini chiles and serve immediately.

Serves 4 to 6

Curry Chicken Salad

3 boneless skinless chicken breasts
Salt and pepper to taste
2 tablespoons olive oil
2/3 cup mayonnaise
2 teaspoons fresh lemon juice
1 1/2 teaspoons curry powder

1/2 cup finely chopped green apple
1/4 cup red grape halves
1/4 cup finely chopped red onion
1/4 cup finely chopped celery
1/4 cup walnuts, chopped
4 cups spring mix

Trim any excess fat from the chicken breasts and season with salt and pepper. Heat the olive oil in a large sauté pan over high heat. Sauté the chicken in the hot oil until golden brown on both sides. Decrease the heat and cook, covered, until the chicken is cooked through. Turn off the heat and let stand until cool.

Combine the mayonnaise, lemon juice and curry powder in a bowl and mix well. Stir in the apple, grapes, onion, celery and walnuts. Chop the chicken and stir into the mayonnaise mixture. Season with salt and pepper. Arrange 1 cup of the spring mix on each of four serving plates and top evenly with the chicken mixture. Serve immediately.

Serves 4

Grilled Cajun Chicken Salad

Buttermilk Ranch Dressing
1/2 cup sour cream
1/4 cup mayonnaise
1/4 cup buttermilk
1 tablespoon chopped fresh parsley
2 garlic cloves, minced
Pinch of cayenne pepper, or to taste
Salt and black pepper to taste

Cajun Seasoning
1 teaspoon garlic powder
1 teaspoon onion powder
1 teaspoon dried thyme

1 teaspoon dried oregano
1 teaspoon paprika
Pinch of cayenne pepper
Salt and black pepper to taste

Salad
6 boneless skinless chicken breasts
1 cup buttermilk
Spring mix
1 cup golden raisins
1 cup pecan pieces
1/2 cup finely chopped celery
1/2 cup finely chopped red onion

To prepare the dressing, combine the sour cream, mayonnaise, buttermilk, parsley, garlic and cayenne pepper in a bowl and mix well. Season with salt and black pepper. Store, covered, in the refrigerator.

To prepare the seasoning, mix the garlic powder, onion powder, thyme, oregano, paprika, cayenne pepper, salt and black pepper in a bowl.

To prepare the salad, rub the chicken breasts with the desired amount of the Cajun seasoning. Arrange the chicken in a single layer in a shallow baking dish. Pour the buttermilk over the chicken and marinate, covered, in the refrigerator for 30 minutes or for up to 10 hours. Remove the chicken from the buttermilk and shake off the excess. Grill the chicken over hot coals until cooked through. Let stand until cool and cut into thin strips.

Mix spring mix, the raisins, pecans, celery and onion in a salad bowl. Add the dressing and toss to coat. Top with the chicken and serve immediately.
Serves 6 to 8

Thai Chicken Salad

Soy Italian Dressing
1 cup Italian salad dressing
2 tablespoons soy sauce
2 teaspoons garlic powder
1 teaspoon ground ginger

Salad
4 boneless skinless chicken breasts
3 tablespoons peanut butter
1/4 cup soy sauce
1 tablespoon honey

1 tablespoon olive oil
1 teaspoon garlic powder
1/2 teaspoon ground ginger
1/4 teaspoon cayenne pepper
Mesclun mix
1 cup drained canned mandarin
    oranges
1 red bell pepper, julienned
3 green onions, thinly sliced
1/3 cup cashews, toasted
1/4 cup fresh cilantro leaves

To prepare the dressing, combine the salad dressing, soy sauce, garlic powder and ginger in a jar with a tight-fitting lid and seal tightly. Shake to mix.

To prepare the salad, trim the excess fat from the chicken. Lightly pound the chicken on a hard surface using a meat mallet. Arrange the chicken in a single layer in a shallow dish. Mix the peanut butter, soy sauce, honey, olive oil, garlic powder, ginger and cayenne pepper in a bowl until blended and spoon over the chicken, turning to coat. Marinate, covered, in the refrigerator for 3 to 24 hours, turning occasionally.

Drain the chicken, reserving the marinade. Grill the chicken over hot coals for about 8 minutes or until cooked through, turning and basting with the reserved marinade. Let stand until cool and cut into 1/2-inch slices. Toss mesclun mix with the dressing in a salad bowl until coated. Top with the chicken and sprinkle with the mandarin oranges, bell pepper, green onions, cashews and cilantro. Serve immediately.
Serves 4

Mesclun mix is a type of salad mix. If it is not available, substitute with chopped romaine.

Chicken and Wild Rice Salad

Dijon Vinaigrette
3/4 cup rice wine vinegar
3 tablespoons Dijon mustard
1 teaspoon sugar
2 garlic cloves, minced
1 1/2 cups canola oil
Salt and pepper to taste

Salad
3 cups cooked wild rice, chilled
2 cups chopped grilled chicken breasts
1 cup cashews
1/2 cup chopped red bell pepper
1/2 cup chopped red onion
1/2 cup golden raisins
2 tablespoons minced green onions

To prepare the vinaigrette, mix the vinegar, Dijon mustard, sugar and garlic in a medium bowl. Add the canola oil gradually, whisking constantly until incorporated. Season with salt and pepper.

To prepare the salad, combine the rice, chicken, cashews, bell pepper, red onion, raisins and green onions in a bowl and mix well. Add the vinaigrette and toss until coated.
Serves 4 to 6

Pesto Chicken Salad

4 boneless skinless chicken breasts
2 tablespoons olive oil
Salt and pepper to taste
1/2 cup mayonnaise
1/4 cup pesto

Grated zest of 2 lemons
1 tablespoon lemon juice
2 teaspoons celery seeds
3 ribs celery, finely chopped

Trim any excess fat from the chicken. Coat the chicken with the olive oil and season with salt and pepper. Grill over hot coals until cooked through. Let stand until cool and chop.

Combine the mayonnaise, pesto, lemon zest, lemon juice and celery seeds in a bowl and mix well. Stir in the chicken and celery; season with salt and pepper. Serve immediately.

Serves 4

Tuna Salad

1 (16-ounce) can tuna, drained
1/2 cup mayonnaise
1/4 cup pickle relish
2 tablespoons spicy mustard
1 tablespoon lemon juice

1 tablespoon dill weed
Grated zest of 1 lemon
1/2 purple onion, finely chopped
3 ribs celery, finely chopped
Salt and pepper to taste

Press the excess moisture from the tuna. Combine the mayonnaise, pickle relish, spicy mustard, lemon juice, dill weed and lemon zest in a bowl and mix well. Stir in the onion and celery. Add the tuna and mix until combined. Season with salt and pepper. Store, covered, in the refrigerator until serving time.

Serves 4 to 6

Shrimp and Avocado Caesar Salad

Croutons
2 cups cubed pumpernickel bread
1 tablespoon unsalted butter, melted
1 tablespoon olive oil
1 teaspoon garlic salt

Shrimp
30 medium shrimp, peeled and
   deveined
Salt and pepper to taste

1/4 cup lemon juice
3 garlic cloves, minced
3 tablespoons olive oil

Salad
Romaine, trimmed and chopped
1/4 cup (1 ounce) shredded Parmesan
   cheese
1 ripe avocado, thinly sliced
Caesar salad dressing to taste

To prepare the croutons, toss the bread cubes with the butter, olive oil and garlic salt in a bowl. Spread in a single layer on a baking sheet and toast at 425 degrees until crisp. Remove to a platter to cool.

To prepare the shrimp, season the shrimp with salt and pepper. Toss the shrimp with the lemon juice, garlic and olive oil in a bowl until coated. Marinate in the refrigerator for 30 minutes, stirring occasionally. Grill over hot coals until the shrimp turn pink, turning occasionally; do not overcook.

To prepare the salad, mix romaine, the cheese, avocado, croutons and shrimp in a large salad bowl. Add salad dressing and toss until coated. Serve immediately.
Serves 6 to 8

Bean Salad

Balsamic Vinaigrette
1/4 cup balsamic vinegar
1 tablespoon orange juice
1 tablespoon chopped fresh parsley
1 tablespoon chopped fresh basil
1 teaspoon chopped fresh oregano
4 garlic cloves, chopped
1/4 cup olive oil
Salt and pepper to taste

Salad
1 (15-ounce) can black beans, drained
    and rinsed
1 (15-ounce) can kidney beans,
    drained and rinsed

1 (15-ounce) can Great Northern
    beans, drained and rinsed
2 cups green beans, cooked, drained
    and chopped
1 (15-ounce) can hearts of palm,
    drained and chopped
1/2 cup finely chopped red bell pepper
1/2 cup finely chopped green
    bell pepper
1/2 cup finely chopped purple onion
2 plum tomatoes, seeded and chopped
2 green onions, sliced

To prepare the vinaigrette, process the vinegar, orange juice, parsley, basil, oregano and garlic in a food processor until puréed. Add the olive oil gradually, processing constantly until incorporated. Season with salt and pepper.

To prepare the salad, combine the beans, hearts of palm, bell peppers, purple onion, tomatoes and green onions in a bowl and mix well. Add the vinaigrette and toss until coated.
Serves 8

If substituting dried herbs for fresh herbs, use half the amount used for fresh.

Black-Eyed Pea Salad

3 cups canned black-eyed peas, drained
1/2 cup chopped yellow onion
1/2 cup chopped red bell pepper
1 teaspoon minced garlic
1/4 cup olive oil

Grated zest and juice of 1 lemon
1 tablespoon chopped fresh basil
1 teaspoon minced fresh rosemary
1 teaspoon minced fresh thyme
Salt and pepper to taste

Combine the peas, onion, bell pepper and garlic in a bowl and mix well. Stir in the olive oil, lemon zest, lemon juice, basil, rosemary and thyme. Season with salt and pepper.
Serves 6

This is a great side dish with grilled fish or chicken.

Creamy Cucumber Salad

1/2 cup sour cream
1/4 cup mayonnaise
3 tablespoons minced
   sun-dried tomatoes
1/4 cup pesto

1 tablespoon chopped green onion
2 cucumbers, seeded and chopped
1/4 purple onion, finely chopped
1/2 red bell pepper, finely chopped
Salt and pepper to taste

Mix the sour cream and mayonnaise in a small bowl until blended. Stir in the tomatoes, pesto and green onion. Toss the cucumbers, purple onion and bell pepper in a bowl. Add enough of the sour cream mixture to the cucumber mixture to coat and mix well. Season with salt and pepper.
Serves 6

Cucumber and Tomato Salad

2 cucumbers, peeled and chopped
1 large tomato, chopped
1 small green bell pepper, finely chopped
1 small purple onion, finely chopped
2 tablespoons chopped fresh basil
1/3 cup vegetable oil
3 tablespoons sugar
3 tablespoons red wine vinegar
3/4 teaspoon salt
1/8 teaspoon pepper
4 cups mixed salad greens
2 cups cubed sourdough bread, toasted

Combine the cucumbers, tomato, bell pepper, onion and basil in a bowl and mix well. Whisk the oil, sugar, vinegar, salt and pepper in a bowl until blended. Add to the cucumber mixture and toss to coat. Marinate, covered, at room temperature for 1 to 4 hours, stirring occasionally.

Divide the salad greens evenly among four plates. Stir the bread cubes into the cucumber mixture and top the greens with an equal portion of the cucumber mixture.
Serves 4

Photograph for this recipe is shown on page 31.

Blue Cheese, Green Apple and Pecan Salad

Spring salad mix
Poppy seed salad dressing to taste
1 Granny Smith apple, sliced
Juice of 1 lemon

1 cup Spiced Pecans (page 197)
1/4 red onion, thinly sliced
1/4 cup crumbled blue cheese

Mix the desired amount of salad greens with the desired amount of salad dressing
in a large salad bowl. Toss the apple with the lemon juice in a small bowl. Add the
apple, pecans, onion and blue cheese to the salad greens and toss to combine.
Serve immediately.
Serves 4 to 6

Fruit and Honey Spinach Salad

Strawberry Dressing
1/4 cup strawberry jam
1/4 cup white wine vinegar
2 tablespoons honey
1 tablespoon orange juice
3/4 cup vegetable oil
Salt and pepper to taste

Salad
Fresh spinach, trimmed and torn
1/4 cup fresh blueberries
1/4 cup quartered fresh strawberries
1/4 cup drained canned mandarin
     orange segments
1 tablespoon sunflower seeds

To prepare the dressing, combine the jam, vinegar, honey and orange juice in
a medium bowl and mix well. Add the oil gradually, whisking constantly until
incorporated. Season with salt and pepper.

To prepare the salad, toss spinach with the dressing in a bowl. Arrange equal
portions of the spinach on each of four plates. Top evenly with the blueberries,
strawberries, mandarin oranges and sunflower seeds. Serve immediately.
Serves 4

Coleslaw

Coleslaw Dressing
1/2 cup mayonnaise
1/4 cup white vinegar
2 tablespoons honey
2 tablespoons Dijon mustard
1 teaspoon celery seeds
Pinch of cayenne pepper

Coleslaw
2 cups shredded green cabbage
2 cups shredded purple cabbage
1/4 cup shredded carrot
1/4 cup grated green apple
1/4 cup grated jicama
1/4 cup shredded purple onion
Salt and pepper to taste

To prepare the dressing, combine the mayonnaise, vinegar, honey, Dijon mustard, celery seeds and cayenne pepper in a bowl and mix well.

To prepare the coleslaw, toss the cabbage, carrot, apple, jicama and onion in a bowl. Add the dressing and mix until coated. Season with salt and pepper.
Serves 4 to 6

You may prepare one day in advance. Store the dressing and coleslaw mixture in separate containers in the refrigerator. Combine the two mixtures just before serving and season with salt and pepper.

Pesto Pizza

1 tablespoon olive oil
1/4 cup finely chopped zucchini
1/4 cup finely chopped yellow squash
1/4 cup finely chopped eggplant
1/4 cup finely chopped purple onion
2 teaspoons chopped garlic
1/2 cup pesto
1/2 cup pizza sauce
1 (12-inch) refrigerator pizza crust
3 plum tomatoes, finely chopped
1 tablespoon chopped fresh basil
1/2 cup (2 ounces) finely chopped fresh mozzarella cheese
Salt and pepper to taste

Heat the olive oil in a large sauté pan over medium-high heat. Sauté the zucchini, yellow squash, eggplant, onion and garlic in the hot oil until the vegetables are brown. Drain and let stand until cool. Mix the pesto and pizza sauce in a small bowl.

Pat the pizza crust over the bottom and up the side of a 12-inch pizza pan sprayed with nonstick cooking spray. Spread the pesto mixture almost to the edge. Layer with the zucchini mixture, tomatoes and basil and sprinkle with the cheese, salt and pepper. Bake at 400 degrees for 12 minutes or until golden brown and bubbly. Cut into wedges and serve immediately.

Serves 6

White Pizza

1 tablespoon olive oil
1 cup chopped hot Italian sausage
1/2 cup chopped zucchini
1/4 cup chopped purple onion
1 teaspoon chopped garlic
1 (12-inch) refrigerator pizza crust
1 cup prepared Alfredo sauce
3 plum tomatoes, finely chopped
1 tablespoon chopped fresh basil
1/2 cup crumbled feta cheese
1/4 cup (1 ounce) shredded Parmesan cheese
1/4 cup (1 ounce) shredded mozzarella cheese
Salt and pepper to taste

Heat the olive oil in a large sauté pan over medium-high heat. Sauté the sausage, zucchini, onion and garlic in the hot oil until the zucchini and onion are brown and the sausage is cooked through; drain. Let stand until cool.

Pat the pizza crust over the bottom and up the side of a 12-inch pizza pan sprayed with nonstick cooking spray. Spread the Alfredo sauce almost to the edge. Layer with the sausage mixture, tomatoes and basil. Sprinkle with the feta cheese, Parmesan cheese, mozzarella cheese, salt and pepper. Bake at 400 degrees for 12 minutes or until golden brown and bubbly. Cut into wedges and serve.
Serves 6

Philly Cheesesteak Sandwiches

2 large hoagie buns, cut lengthwise into halves
1/4 cup olive oil
1/2 red bell pepper, thinly sliced
1/2 green bell pepper, thinly sliced
1 small yellow onion, cut into halves and thinly sliced
1 cup button mushrooms, thinly sliced
1 (10-ounce) rib-eye steak, thinly sliced
Salt and pepper to taste
2 tablespoons Worcestershire sauce
2 slices Swiss cheese
2 slices provolone cheese
1/4 cup mayonnaise

Brush the cut sides of the buns with a small amount of the olive oil. Arrange the bun halves cut side up on a baking sheet and broil for 1 minute or until golden brown. Heat the remaining olive oil in a nonstick skillet over medium-high heat and add the bell peppers, onion and mushrooms. Cook for 3 to 4 minutes or until the vegetables begin to soften and brown around the edges, stirring frequently.

Add the steak to the onion mixture and cook for 2 to 3 minutes or to the desired degree of doneness. Season with salt and pepper and drizzle with the Worcestershire sauce. Turn off the heat and lay the Swiss cheese and provolone cheese over the steak mixture. Spread the mayonnaise over the toasted sides of the buns. Divide the steak mixture between the two buns and serve immediately.
Makes 2 sandwiches

To make a Philly Chicken Sandwich, substitute 10 ounces boneless skinless chicken breasts for the rib-eye steak.

Roast Beef and Blue Cheese Sandwiches

Herb Mayonnaise
1 cup mayonnaise
1 tablespoon chopped fresh basil
1 teaspoon chopped fresh cilantro
1 teaspoon chopped fresh Italian parsley

Sandwiches
8 slices sourdough sandwich bread, toasted
12 thin slices roast beef
1/2 cup crumbled blue cheese
2 roasted red bell peppers, thinly sliced
4 leaves romaine
8 thin slices tomato

To prepare the herb mayonnaise, combine the mayonnaise, basil, cilantro and parsley in a bowl and mix well. Store, covered, in the refrigerator.

To prepare the sandwiches, spread the herb mayonnaise on one side of each slice of bread. Layer half the bread slices evenly with the roast beef, cheese, bell peppers, romaine and tomato. Top with the remaining bread slices mayonnaise side down. Cut each sandwich diagonally into halves and serve immediately.
Makes 4 sandwiches

Spicy Roast Beef Subs with Tomato Garlic Sauce

2 cups beef stock
2 tablespoons ketchup
1 1/2 tablespoons Worcestershire sauce
2 garlic cloves, minced
1/2 teaspoon dried basil
1/2 teaspoon dried oregano
Pinch of cayenne pepper, or to taste
1 pound roast beef, thinly sliced
6 hoagie buns, cut lengthwise into halves
1/4 cup (1/2 stick) unsalted butter, melted
12 slices Swiss cheese

Bring the stock, ketchup, Worcestershire sauce, garlic, basil, oregano and cayenne pepper to a boil in a medium saucepan. Reduce the heat to low and simmer for 5 minutes, stirring occasionally. Add the roast beef to the ketchup mixture and mix well. Let stand for 5 minutes to allow the roast beef to soak up the sauce. Drain, reserving the sauce.

Brush the cut sides of the buns with the butter and arrange butter side up on a baking sheet. Broil until golden brown. Divide the roast beef evenly among the buns and top with the cheese. Cut the sandwiches into halves and serve with the reserved sauce.

Makes 6 subs

Meatball Sandwiches

Marinara Sauce
2 tablespoons olive oil
3 garlic cloves, minced
1 tablespoon minced fresh parsley
1 teaspoon minced fresh oregano
1 teaspoon minced fresh basil
Pinch of crushed red pepper flakes
4 cups canned crushed tomatoes
Salt and black pepper to taste

Sandwiches
1 pound ground beef
1 cup Italian-seasoned bread crumbs

1/4 cup minced yellow onion
1/4 cup minced green bell pepper
2 eggs, lightly beaten
1 tablespoon Worcestershire sauce
1 garlic clove, crushed
Pinch of crushed red pepper flakes
Salt and black pepper to taste
6 to 8 hoagie buns, cut lengthwise into
    halves and toasted
1 cup (4 ounces) shredded
    Parmesan cheese
1 1/2 cups (6 ounces) shredded
    mozzarella cheese

To prepare the sauce, heat a medium saucepan over medium heat and add the olive oil and garlic. Cook until the garlic begins to sizzle and then stir in the parsley, oregano, basil and red pepper flakes. Cook for 30 seconds. Stir in the tomatoes and simmer for 30 minutes, stirring occasionally. Season with salt and black pepper.

To prepare the sandwiches, combine the ground beef, bread crumbs, onion, bell pepper, eggs, Worcestershire sauce, garlic, red pepper flakes, salt and black pepper in a bowl and mix well. Shape the ground beef mixture into small meatballs. Arrange the meatballs on a baking sheet sprayed with nonstick cooking spray. Bake at 450 degrees for 12 minutes or until the meatballs are cooked through; drain.

Divide the meatballs evenly among the bottom halves of the hoagie buns and top evenly with the sauce, Parmesan cheese and mozzarella cheese. Arrange on a baking sheet and broil just until the cheese melts. Replace the top halves of the buns. Let stand for 3 minutes and cut each sandwich into halves. Serve immediately.
Makes 6 to 8 sandwiches

If time is of the essence, use commercially-prepared marinara sauce and frozen meatballs.

Maple Bacon, Tomato and Avocado Cheese Sandwiches

2 tablespoons mayonnaise
Grated zest of 1 lemon
4 slices whole grain bread
2 tablespoons unsalted butter, softened
4 slices sharp Cheddar cheese
4 slices maple bacon, crisp-cooked and drained
1 avocado, sliced
4 slices Muenster cheese
1 beefsteak tomato, sliced

Mix the mayonnaise and lemon zest in a small bowl. Spread the mayonnaise mixture evenly on one side of each of the four slices of bread. Spread the butter evenly on the remaining sides of the bread.

Layer two slices of the bread mayonnaise side up evenly with the Cheddar cheese, bacon, avocado, Muenster cheese and tomato. Top with the remaining bread slices butter side up. Cook in a large nonstick skillet or on a griddle over medium heat for 2 to 3 minutes per side or until the sandwiches are golden brown and the cheese melts.
Makes 2 sandwiches

Muffuletta

1 (12-ounce) jar pickled vegetables, drained and chopped
1/4 cup green olives, chopped
1/4 cup kalamata olives, pitted and chopped
3/4 cup mayonnaise
1 tablespoon lemon juice
1/2 teaspoon dried Italian seasoning
1/2 teaspoon dried crushed red pepper
6 thin slices cooked ham
6 thin slices salami
6 thin slices mortadella
6 ounces provolone cheese, sliced
1 (12-inch) round loaf bread, split into halves

Combine the pickled vegetables, green olives and kalamata olives in a bowl and mix well. Stir in the mayonnaise, lemon juice, Italian seasoning and red pepper.

Layer the ham, salami, mortadella and cheese evenly on the bottom half of the bread loaf. Top with the remaining bread half and wrap in plastic wrap. Chill in the refrigerator. Slice as desired.

Serves 6

This sandwich is great for traveling and can be made in advance and stored in the refrigerator.

Italian Club Sandwiches

1/3 cup mayonnaise
1/3 cup Dijon mustard
12 slices white bread, toasted
8 leaves leaf lettuce
8 slices tomato
4 slices mozzarella cheese
4 slices Provolone cheese
8 slices cooked ham
4 slices salami
4 slices mortadella

Mix the mayonnaise and Dijon mustard in a bowl. Spread about 2 teaspoons of the mayonnaise mixture on one side of each bread slice.

For each sandwich, layer 1 slice of the bread mayonnaise side up with 2 leaves of the lettuce, 2 slices of the tomato, 1 slice of the mozzarella cheese and 1 slice of the Provolone cheese. Top with another slice of the bread, 2 slices of the ham, 1 slice of the salami and 1 slice of the mortadella. Finish the sandwiches by topping with the remaining slices of bread mayonnaise side down. Secure with wooden picks and cut into halves.
Makes 4 sandwiches

Salami, Provolone and Ham Sandwiches with Caper Relish

Caper Relish
1 tablespoon minced seeded
   pepperoncini chile
1 tablespoon minced capers
1 tablespoon minced green olives
1 tablespoon minced pimento
1 tablespoon minced yellow onion
1 tablespoon olive oil
1 teaspoon minced fresh oregano

Sandwiches
4 slices sourdough bread
2 slices provolone cheese
4 thin slices salami
4 thin slices cooked ham
2 leaves romaine
4 slices tomato

To prepare the relish, combine the pepperoncini chile, capers, olives, pimento, onion, olive oil and oregano in a bowl and mix well.

To prepare the sandwiches, spread the relish evenly on one side of each slice of bread. Layer the cheese, salami, ham, romaine and tomato on the relish side of two slices of the bread. Top with the remaining bread slices relish side down. Cut each sandwich into halves and serve immediately.
Makes 2 sandwiches

Club Sandwiches with Olive Cream Cheese

Olive Cream Cheese
4 ounces cream cheese, softened
1/4 cup minced pimento-stuffed
   green olives
1 tablespoon mayonnaise
1 tablespoon minced yellow onion
1 tablespoon prepared horseradish
Pinch of garlic powder
Pepper to taste

Sandwiches
12 slices white sandwich bread, toasted
8 slices tomato
12 thin slices turkey
4 slices Swiss cheese
8 slices bacon, crisp-cooked
   and drained
4 leaves romaine

To prepare the olive cream cheese, combine the cream cheese, olives, mayonnaise, onion, horseradish and garlic powder in a mixing bowl or food processor and beat or process until combined. Season with pepper.

To prepare the sandwiches, divide the bread slices into four stacks. Spread the olive cream cheese over one slice of each stack using half the mixture. Top each with 2 slices of the tomato, 3 slices of the turkey and 1 slice of the Swiss cheese. Layer each with 1 slice of the remaining bread from each stack. Spread these bread slices with the remaining cream cheese mixture and layer evenly with the bacon and romaine. Top with the remaining bread slices and secure each sandwich with four long wooden picks. Cut into quarters and serve immediately.

Makes 4 sandwiches

Smoked Turkey, Bacon and Grilled Apple Wraps

Guacamole
2 ripe avocados, finely chopped
1/4 red onion, minced
1 jalapeño chile, seeded and minced
2 tablespoons chopped fresh cilantro
1 tablespoon lime juice
1 tablespoon olive oil
Salt and pepper to taste

Wraps
1 large Green apple, thinly sliced
1/2 red onion, thinly sliced or separated
    into rings

2 tablespoons olive oil
2 tablespoons mayonnaise
2 tablespoons Dijon mustard
4 large flour tortillas
8 slices tomato
12 thin slices turkey
4 leaves romaine
8 slices bacon, crisp-cooked
    and drained
Salt and pepper to taste

To prepare the guacamole, combine the avocados, onion, jalapeño chile, cilantro, lime juice and olive oil in a bowl and mix until the desired consistency. Season with salt and pepper.

To prepare the wraps, toss the apple and onion with the olive oil in a bowl. Sauté the apple mixture in a sauté pan over medium-high heat for 2 to 3 minutes or until golden brown and tender. Mix the mayonnaise and Dijon mustard in a bowl.

Spread one side of each tortilla evenly with the mayonnaise mixture and then with the guacamole. Divide the apple mixture among the tortillas and top each with 2 slices of the tomato, 3 slices of the turkey, 1 romaine leaf and 2 slices of the bacon. Sprinkle with salt and pepper. Roll the tortillas to enclose the filling and cut into halves.

Makes 4 wraps

Turkey Sausage Sandwiches

6 Italian turkey sausages
1 1/2 cups sauerkraut, drained
2 tablespoons olive oil
2 large red onions, thinly sliced
4 long green Italian sweet chiles, seeded and thinly sliced
2 red bell peppers, cut lengthwise into 1/4-inch strips
Salt and pepper to taste
6 wheat hoagie buns, split and toasted
2 tablespoons Dijon mustard
2 tablespoons mayonnaise
12 slices reduced-fat Swiss cheese

Cut each sausage lengthwise into halves. Fry the sausages in a large sauté pan over medium heat for 4 to 5 minutes per side or until crisp and cooked through, turning once. Drain and cover to keep warm. Heat the sauerkraut in a small saucepan and cover to keep warm.

Heat the olive oil in a sauté pan over medium-high heat. Cook the onions in the hot oil for 7 to 8 minutes or until limp and light brown, turning frequently with a spatula. Add the sweet chiles and bell peppers and cook for 5 minutes longer, stirring frequently. Season with salt and pepper.

Spread the cut sides of the buns evenly with the Dijon mustard and mayonnaise. Top the bottom halves of the buns with equal portions of the onion mixture and sausage halves. Layer evenly with the sauerkraut and cheese. Arrange on a baking sheet cheese side up and broil just until the cheese melts. Top with the remaining bun tops and cut into halves. Serve immediately.

Makes 6 sandwiches

Grilled Mexican Chicken Sandwiches

Lime Cilantro Mayonnaise
$1/2$ cup sour cream
$1/2$ cup mayonnaise
1 tablespoon lime juice
1 tablespoon chopped fresh cilantro
Salt to taste

Sandwiches
8 boneless skinless chicken breasts,
    trimmed
3 tablespoons olive oil

4 garlic cloves, minced
$1^{1}/2$ teaspoons chili powder
$1/2$ teaspoon salt
$1/2$ teaspoon cayenne pepper
8 slices Pepper Jack cheese
1 avocado, thinly sliced
1 tablespoon lime juice
8 sandwich buns, split and
    toasted
Romaine, chopped
2 cups salsa

To prepare the lime cilantro mayonnaise, combine the sour cream, mayonnaise, lime juice and cilantro in a bowl and mix well. Season with salt. Chill, covered, for 1 hour or for up to 1 week.

To prepare the sandwiches, pound the chicken between sheets of waxed paper with a meat mallet until flattened. Mix the olive oil, garlic, chili powder, salt and cayenne pepper in a bowl.

Rub the surface of the chicken with the olive oil mixture and arrange the chicken in a single layer in a shallow dish. Marinate, covered, for 1 to 10 hours. Grill over hot coals until cooked through, turning occasionally. Remove the chicken to a platter and top each piece with 1 slice of the cheese.

Toss the avocado with the lime juice in a bowl. Spread the cut sides of each bun with some of the lime cilantro mayonnaise. Layer the bottom halves of the buns equally with the chicken, romaine, salsa and avocado. Top with the remaining bun tops and serve immediately.

Makes 8 sandwiches

For a low-carb option, enjoy the filling without the bread.

Chicken Teriyaki Sandwiches

Teriyaki Sauce
1 cup soy sauce
3/4 cup packed brown sugar
2 tablespoons sesame oil
Juice of 1 orange
Juice of 1 lime
2 garlic cloves, minced
1 tablespoon minced fresh ginger
1/2 teaspoon crushed red pepper
1/4 cup water

2 tablespoons cornstarch
Salt and black pepper to taste

Chicken
4 boneless skinless chicken breasts
Leaf lettuce
4 slices tomato
4 pineapple rings
4 kaiser rolls, split and toasted

To prepare the sauce, combine the soy sauce, brown sugar, sesame oil, orange juice, lime juice, garlic, ginger and red pepper in a small saucepan and mix well. Bring to a boil and reduce the heat to low. Simmer for 5 minutes, stirring occasionally.

Mix the water and cornstarch in a small bowl. Gradually pour the cornstarch mixture into the warm sauce, whisking constantly. Bring to a boil and boil for 2 minutes; remove from the heat. Season with salt and black pepper.

To prepare the sandwiches, arrange the chicken in a shallow dish and cover with the teriyaki sauce, turning to coat. Marinate, covered, in the refrigerator for 4 to 10 hours, turning occasionally. Grill the chicken over hot coals until cooked through, turning occasionally. Divide the lettuce, tomato, pineapple and chicken evenly among the rolls. Cut each sandwich into halves and serve immediately.
Makes 4 sandwiches

Shrimp Po' Boys with Rémoulade Sauce

Rémoulade Sauce

1 cup mayonnaise
1/4 cup ketchup
1/4 cup Creole mustard
1 tablespoon minced celery
1 tablespoon minced yellow onion
1 tablespoon chopped green onions
1 teaspoon hot red pepper sauce
1/2 teaspoon minced garlic
Salt and pepper to taste

Po' Boys

2 cups buttermilk
20 medium shrimp, peeled
   and deveined
1 1/2 cups yellow cornmeal
1/2 cup all-purpose flour
1/2 teaspoon salt
1/2 teaspoon freshly ground pepper
Vegetable oil for frying
4 French bread rolls, split lengthwise
1 cup shredded romaine
8 slices tomato

To prepare the sauce, combine the mayonnaise, ketchup, Creole mustard, celery, yellow onion, green onions, hot sauce, garlic, salt and pepper in a bowl and mix well.

To prepare the Po' Boys, pour the buttermilk over the shrimp in a large shallow dish or combine in a sealable plastic bag. Cover or seal and chill for 2 hours or longer; drain.

Mix the cornmeal, flour, salt and pepper in a shallow dish. Coat the shrimp with the flour mixture and tap the shrimp lightly to remove any excess. Heat enough oil in a deep skillet to cover the shrimp. Fry the shrimp in batches in the hot oil until golden brown and cooked through; drain.

Spread the cut sides of the rolls with the rémoulade sauce. Layer the bottom halves evenly with romaine, tomato and shrimp. Drizzle with any remaining sauce and top with the roll tops. Serve with lemon wedges.

Makes 4 Po-Boys

Oysters can easily be substituted for the shrimp for Oyster Po' Boys. Or, you can use a combination of both shrimp and oysters for a delicious variation. The Rémoulade Sauce may be a bit spicy for some. An easy way to please everyone is to decrease the amount of hot sauce added to the Rémoulade Sauce and serve the sandwich with a bottle of hot sauce on the side.

Tarragon Egg Salad Sandwiches

6 hard-cooked eggs, chopped
2 tablespoons finely chopped celery
1 tablespoon chopped fresh tarragon
1 tablespoon grated yellow onion
1/4 cup mayonnaise
1/2 teaspoon Dijon mustard
1/4 teaspoon salt
1/8 teaspoon freshly ground pepper
8 slices wheat sandwich bread
4 slices tomato
4 leaves romaine

Combine the eggs, celery, tarragon and onion in a bowl and mix well. Stir in the mayonnaise, Dijon mustard, salt and pepper. Chill, covered, for 4 hours. Taste and season with additional salt and pepper if needed.

Spread the egg salad evenly on 4 slices of the bread. Layer with the tomato, romaine and remaining slices of bread. Cut each sandwich into halves and serve.

Makes 4 sandwiches

Eggplant Parmesan Sandwiches

1 eggplant, cut into 1/8-inch slices
Salt and pepper to taste
1 cup panko
1/2 cup (2 ounces) grated Parmesan cheese
1 tablespoon Italian seasoning
2 eggs, lightly beaten
Vegetable oil for frying
1 loaf crusty French bread, split lengthwise into halves
2 cups spaghetti sauce
1 1/2 cups (6 ounces) shredded mozzarella cheese

Sprinkle both sides of the eggplant slices with salt and pepper. Mix the bread crumbs, Parmesan cheese and Italian seasoning in a shallow dish. Dip the eggplant in the eggs and coat with the bread crumb mixture. Fry the coated eggplant in oil in a large skillet over medium-high heat until golden brown on each side; drain.

Spread the cut sides of the bread loaf heavily with the sauce. Arrange the eggplant on the bottom half and sprinkle with the cheese. Keeping the sandwich open-faced, arrange the bread halves on a baking sheet and broil until the cheese melts. Replace the top bread half and cut into six equal portions.

Makes 6 sandwiches

Cheese-Stuffed Portobello Mushroom Sandwiches

1 cup plus 2 tablespoons olive oil
6 tablespoons aged balsamic vinegar
3 garlic cloves, minced
1/4 yellow onion, minced
Salt and freshly ground pepper to taste
6 portobello mushrooms, stems removed
1 cup oil-pack sun-dried tomatoes, drained
1/2 cup pine nuts
12 fresh basil leaves
6 sourdough rolls, cut into halves
1 1/2 cups crumbled goat cheese
1/2 cup (2 ounces) grated Parmesan cheese

Whisk the olive oil, vinegar, garlic, onion, salt and pepper in a small bowl. Arrange the mushroom caps in a single layer in a shallow dish. Pour half the olive oil mixture over the mushrooms, reserving the remaining olive oil mixture. Marinate the mushrooms, covered, at room temperature for 1 hour, turning after 30 minutes.

Arrange the mushrooms on a lightly oiled grill rack over hot coals and weight down with a large skillet. Grill the mushrooms for about 4 minutes or until tender and seared on both sides. Process the sun-dried tomatoes, pine nuts, basil and remaining olive oil mixture in a food processor or blender until puréed.

Spoon the sun-dried tomato mixture on the cut sides of the roll tops. Sprinkle evenly with the goat cheese and Parmesan cheese. Arrange one mushroom on the bottom half of each roll and place the halves together. Secure each sandwich with wooden picks and cut into halves. Serve immediately.
Makes 6 sandwiches

Tomato, Basil and Mozzarella Sandwiches

4 (1/2-inch) slices sourdough bread, toasted
Olive oil for brushing
1/4 cup mayonnaise
4 slices mozzarella cheese
6 slices tomato
2 teaspoons balsamic vinegar
4 fresh basil leaves
Sea salt or kosher salt to taste
Coarse pepper to taste

Brush one side of each bread slice with olive oil. Spread the mayonnaise over the olive oil on 2 slices of the bread. Layer with the cheese, tomato, vinegar and basil. Sprinkle with salt and pepper and top with the remaining 2 slices of bread. Cut into halves and serve immediately.
Makes 2 sandwiches

Dinner

Avocado Soup with Shrimp and Tomato Salsa

Asparagus Soup with Parmesan Custards

Carrot and Ginger Soup

Corn Chowder

Roasted Eggplant Soup

Summer Gazpacho

Creamy Tomato and Bacon Soup

Vidalia Onion Soup

Dry-Rubbed Rib-Eye Steak with Barbeque Sauce

Grilled Flank Steak with Caribbean Rice

Lasagna

Cheese and Mushroom Meat Loaf with Buttermilk Mashed Potatoes

Spaghetti and Bolognese Sauce

Molasses-Glazed Pork Roast with Black Pepper Dumplings

Roasted Pork Loin with Raspberry Chipotle Glaze

Blackened Pork Chops with Pineapple Mint Chutney and Corn Fritters

Roasted Pork Chops with Apple Cider Glaze and Mashed Root Vegetables

Pancetta-Wrapped Pork Chops with Tomato-Mustard Seed Chutney and Dijon Mashed Potatoes

Coconut Chicken with African Spices and Couscous

Sautéed Chicken with Harissa Sauce and Couscous

Chicken Piccata with Parmesan-Herb Polenta and Wilted Spinach

Sautéed Chicken with Cheddar Spinach Grits

Thai Chicken with Sweet Chile-Garlic Sauce and Cilantro Lime Rice

Lime Cilantro Chicken with Chili Butter

Orecchiette with Chicken

Crab Meat-Stuffed Flounder

Grilled Salmon with Black Bean Salsa and Chipotle Orange Vinaigrette

Poached Salmon with Lemon Butter Sauce and Sour Cream-Dill Mashed Potatoes

Red Snapper Tacos

Tilapia Amandine with Creole Meunière Sauce

Blackened Tuna and Roasted Vegetable Salsa with Smoked Corn Sauce

Grilled Tuna with Pecan Lime Butter

Crispy Crab Cakes with Mango and Green Onion Relish

Fettuccini with Sea Scallops

Shrimp and Artichokes over Parmesan Grits

Panko-Fried Shrimp with Orange Chipotle Hollandaise Sauce and Lemon Orange Rice

Low-Country Boil with Lemon Butter and Cocktail Sauce

Louisiana-Style Barbecued Shrimp with Corn Maque Choux

Seafood Stew

Curried Broccoli

Braised Red Cabbage

Grilled Corn on the Cob with Spiced Butter

Steamed Green Beans with Blistered Tomatoes

Roasted Rosemary Red Potatoes

Acorn Squash Risotto with Spinach and Bacon

Four-Cheese Risotto

Three-Cheese Grits

Buttermilk Biscuits

Dinner Corn Bread

Dinner Recipes from the Café

Elliott Loving

One Saturday, Julie and I were making our way to the fountain in Forsyth Park when we ran into Elliott Loving, who was making his way home from work. Dressed in his white chef coat and wearing the checkered pants worn by those in the industry, Elliott smiled broadly when he saw me. We greeted one another with an embrace and I asked him how he was doing.

"Good," he replied with a grin. "Very good."

It had not been too long ago when things had not been so good. Homeless and living at Inner City Night Shelter, Elliott simply could not get things together. He did make his way to the Employment & Training Center, but floundered in the Landscape Management class. Staff would not give up on him, however, so they referred him to the Culinary Arts Training Program.

I met him several weeks later when he was in the Starfish Café. The first impression was not a good one. Elliott was like many homeless people and would not look you in the eyes if you addressed him. His handshake was nothing more than an extended limp hand. I didn't think that the future held much for him.

As these students have often done, I was again proven wrong. Over the nine weeks that he was in the café, Elliott went through a transformation that was nothing short of miraculous. A light came on behind his eyes, and he loved showing it off. Suddenly, he held my gaze with beaming eyes. His voice deepened when he spoke to me. His handshake grew firm and confident.

At the graduation ceremony, Elliott was one of only three students who prepared to receive his certificate. Seventeen students had begun, but only these three survived. Elliott's smile lit the room at Savannah Tech.

Chef Bob announced that when someone graduates from culinary school, they are given Le Cordon Bleu Medal. Le Cordon Bleu, I have now learned, was the first culinary arts school in France, and now graduates throughout the world are recognized with the medal. All except graduates of the Starfish Café!

"So," Chef Bob explained, "today we begin a new tradition." He held up a starfish carved from wood and hanging on a ribbon. "Today, you are the first graduates to receive Le Cordon Bleu Starfish Medal!"

Everyone laughed and clapped. I watched Elliott, whose smile added to the brilliance of the room. When Chef Bob hung the medal around his neck, I found myself filled with emotion. After the ceremony, I hugged Elliott in congratulations.

"I have a job!" he beamed.

So on that Saturday night in Forsyth Park, Elliott explained that he loved his work at Elizabeth on 37th.

"Things are just very, very good," he told me. "I love working there."

I congratulated him and he continued down the sidewalk.

A couple of days later, I was being interviewed by a Savannah State student about my leadership style. She asked me why I choose to do this kind of work. After a thoughtful moment, I told her about Elliott Loving.

Avocado Soup with Shrimp and Tomato Salsa

Soup
4 large avocados, chopped
1 cucumber, peeled, seeded
    and chopped
3 cups vegetable broth
3/4 cup reduced-fat sour cream
3/4 cup (about) milk
2 tablespoons lemon juice
Salt and pepper to taste

Tomato Salsa and Assembly
1 1/2 cups finely chopped tomatoes
1/3 cup minced red onion
1/4 cup chopped fresh cilantro
1/4 cup olive oil
3 tablespoons lime juice, or to taste
2 or 3 jalapeño chiles, seeded
    and minced
2 garlic cloves, minced
Salt and freshly ground pepper to taste
12 to 16 steamed shrimp, peeled,
    deveined and chopped

To prepare the soup, process the avocados, cucumber, broth and sour cream in batches in a blender until puréed, adding the milk as needed for a desirable soup consistency. Pour the avocado mixture into a bowl and stir in the lemon juice, salt and pepper. Chill, covered, for 1 hour or just until cold.

To prepare the salsa, combine the tomatoes, onion, cilantro, olive oil, lime juice, jalapeño chiles and garlic in a bowl and mix well. Season with salt and pepper. Taste the chilled soup and adjust the seasonings. Ladle the soup into chilled bowls and top each serving with one-fourth of the shrimp and a generous spoonful of the salsa.
Serves 4

If time is of the essence, purchase commercially-prepared salsa.

Asparagus Soup with Parmesan Custards

Parmesan Custards
1 cup heavy cream
1/4 cup milk
1/3 cup coarsely grated
    Parmesan cheese
1 egg
2 egg yolks
Pinch of salt
Pinch of white pepper

Soup and Assembly
1 1/2 pounds asparagus spears
1/4 cup (1/2 stick) butter
1 yellow onion, chopped
3 garlic cloves, minced
1/4 cup dry vermouth
3 cups (or more) chicken stock
Pinch of cayenne pepper
Pinch of ground nutmeg
Salt and freshly ground black pepper
    to taste
3/4 cup heavy cream

To prepare the custards, bring the cream, milk and cheese to a boil in a heavy saucepan, stirring occasionally. Remove from the heat and steep, covered, for 30 minutes to allow the flavors to blend. Pour the steeped cream mixture through a fine mesh strainer into a bowl, pressing lightly on the cheese solids to extract all the liquid; discard the solids.

Whisk the egg, egg yolks, salt and white pepper in a bowl until blended. Add the steeped cream gradually, whisking constantly until smooth. Divide the cream mixture among four to six greased soufflé cups. Arrange the soufflé cups in a 9×13-inch baking pan. Fill the baking pan with enough warm water to reach three-fourths of the way up the sides of the cups. Place the pan on the center oven rack and bake at 300 degrees for 30 to 40 minutes or until set. Remove the cups to a wire rack and let stand for 5 minutes. Run a thin knife around the edge of each cup to loosen the custards and invert the custards onto a baking sheet lined with waxed paper.

To prepare the soup, snap off the woody ends of the asparagus spears and discard. Chop the spears into 1-inch pieces. Melt the butter in a heavy saucepan over medium heat and add the onion and garlic. Sauté for 3 to 4 minutes or until the onion is tender. Add the vermouth and cook until most of the liquid evaporates. Stir in the asparagus, stock, cayenne pepper, nutmeg, salt and black pepper.

Bring to a simmer and reduce the heat to medium-low. Cook, covered, for 20 minutes or until the asparagus is tender, stirring occasionally. Purée the soup using an immersion blender for about 2 minutes or until smooth. Press the soup through a fine mesh strainer into a clean saucepan; discard the solids. Stir in the cream and additional stock if desired for the desired consistency. Season with salt and black pepper and reheat over low heat. Place one custard in the bottom of each soup bowl and ladle the hot soup over the custards. Serve immediately.
Serves 4 to 6

Carrot and Ginger Soup

1/4 cup canola oil
1 yellow onion, chopped
2 ribs celery, chopped
1/2 cup grated fresh ginger
6 cups chopped peeled carrots
5 cups chicken broth
1 cup apple juice
2 tablespoons salt
1 teaspoon ground coriander
1/2 teaspoon ground pepper

Heat the canola oil in a large saucepan over medium heat and add the onion, celery and ginger. Cook for 7 minutes, stirring frequently. Stir in the carrots, broth, apple juice, salt, coriander and pepper and bring to a boil. Reduce the heat to low.

Simmer for 20 minutes or until the carrots are tender. Process the soup in a blender or food processor until puréed. Ladle into soup bowls and garnish with parsley.

Serves 6

Corn Chowder

1 tablespoon unsalted butter
1 tablespoon olive oil
1 yellow onion, chopped
1/4 cup minced celery
Kernels of 12 ears of corn
1/2 cup finely chopped ham
2 garlic cloves, minced
2 tablespoons chopped fresh parsley
1 teaspoon chopped fresh thyme
Pinch of cayenne pepper
Pinch of ground nutmeg
6 cups milk
1 tablespoon Worcestershire sauce
2 russet potatoes, peeled and chopped
Salt and black pepper to taste

Heat the butter and olive oil in a large heavy saucepan until the butter melts. Cook the onion and celery in the hot butter mixture for 4 minutes or until the onion is tender. Stir in the corn, ham, garlic, parsley, thyme, cayenne pepper and nutmeg.

Cook for 3 minutes, stirring occasionally. Stir in the milk, Worcestershire sauce and potatoes and simmer for 30 minutes or until the potatoes are tender. Process the soup in batches in a blender or food processor until puréed. Return the soup to the saucepan and simmer just until heated through. Season with salt and black pepper and ladle into soup bowls.
Serves 6

Roasted Eggplant Soup

2 large eggplant
Olive oil for brushing
2 tablespoons olive oil
1 yellow onion, finely chopped
1 leek bulb, finely chopped
2 ribs celery, finely chopped
4 garlic cloves, minced
5 cups chicken broth
1 cup heavy cream

Pinch of cayenne pepper
Pinch of ground nutmeg
2 pita bread rounds
2 tablespoons olive oil
1/2 cup crumbled goat cheese
Salt and black pepper to taste
2 tablespoons chopped fresh
    Italian parsley

Brush the eggplant with olive oil and arrange on a baking sheet. Bake at 425 degrees for 20 to 25 minutes or until brownish-black on the outside and tender on the inside when pierced with a fork. Let stand until cool. Peel and chop the eggplant.

Heat 2 tablespoons olive oil in a stockpot over medium heat. Add the onion, leek, celery and garlic and cook for 4 minutes or until the onion is tender. Stir in the eggplant, broth, cream, cayenne pepper and nutmeg and bring to a simmer. Cook for 30 minutes, stirring occasionally.

Cut each pita round into four triangles and brush the tops with 2 tablespoons olive oil. Sprinkle with the goat cheese and arrange on a baking sheet. Broil until the cheese is golden brown and the pita chips are crisp. Remove to a wire rack.

Process the soup in batches in a blender until puréed. Return the soup to the stockpot and bring to a simmer. Season with salt and black pepper. Ladle into soup bowls and sprinkle with the parsley. Serve with the pita chips.

Serves 4

Summer Gazpacho

3 pounds plum tomatoes, seeded and chopped
1/2 cup red wine vinegar
1/2 cup olive oil
1/4 cup fresh basil
Grated zest and juice of 2 limes
1 tablespoon chopped Italian parsley
1/2 teaspoon Tabasco sauce
1 quart (4 cups) tomato juice
1 small red onion, finely chopped
1 cucumber, peeled, seeded and finely chopped
1 red bell pepper, finely chopped
2 ribs celery, finely chopped
4 scallions, finely chopped
2 teaspoons Worcestershire sauce
Salt and pepper to taste

Process the tomatoes, vinegar, olive oil, basil, lime zest, lime juice, parsley and Tabasco sauce in a food processor until puréed. Pour the puréed mixture into a large bowl and stir in the tomato juice, onion, cucumber, bell pepper, celery, scallions and Worcestershire sauce. Season with salt and pepper. Chill, covered, for 2 to 10 hours before serving.

Serves 6

Creamy Tomato and Bacon Soup

2 tablespoons olive oil
8 slices bacon, finely chopped
1 yellow onion, finely chopped
2 ribs celery, finely chopped
3 garlic cloves, chopped
8 red tomatoes, peeled and
    cut into quarters
2 cups chicken broth
1/2 cup heavy cream
1 tablespoon finely chopped
    fresh oregano

1/2 teaspoon sugar
1/2 teaspoon red pepper flakes
1/4 cup arborio rice
Salt and freshly ground black pepper
    to taste
8 baguette slices
Olive oil for brushing
1/4 cup crumbled blue cheese
1/4 cup (1 ounce) grated
    Parmesan cheese

Heat 2 tablespoons olive oil in a large saucepan over medium heat. Cook the bacon in the hot oil for 3 minutes, stirring frequently. Reduce the heat to low and stir in the onion, celery and garlic. Cook for 4 minutes or until the onion is tender. Stir in the tomatoes, broth, cream, oregano, sugar and red pepper flakes and bring to a simmer; do not boil. Add the rice and mix well.

Cook for 30 minutes or until the rice is tender. Purée the soup in batches in a blender or food processor. Return the soup to the saucepan and bring to a simmer. Season with salt and black pepper.

Brush the baguette slices with olive oil and arrange on a baking sheet. Sprinkle evenly with the blue cheese and Parmesan cheese. Broil just until the cheese is golden brown. Ladle the soup into bowls and serve with the cheese-topped baguette slices.

Serves 4

Vidalia Onion Soup

2 tablespoons olive oil
4 large Vidalia onions, thinly sliced
1/2 cup dry white wine
6 cups chicken broth
2 teaspoons chopped fresh thyme
2 bay leaves
2 teaspoons salt
1 teaspoon freshly ground pepper
1 cup (4 ounces) grated Gruyère cheese

Heat the olive oil in a saucepan over medium heat and add the onions. Cook for 10 minutes or until the onions are brown, adjusting the heat as needed to prevent burning. Stir in the wine. Add the broth, thyme, bay leaves, salt and pepper and mix well.

Simmer for about 25 minutes, stirring occasionally. Discard the bay leaves and ladle into soup bowls. Sprinkle evenly with the cheese.
Serves 6

Dry-Rubbed Rib-Eye Steak with Barbecue Sauce

Dry Rub
1 tablespoon chili powder
1 tablespoon ground cumin
1 tablespoon ground coriander
2 teaspoons dry mustard
2 teaspoons dried oregano
1 teaspoon cayenne pepper

3 tablespoons red wine vinegar
2 tablespoons brown sugar
1 tablespoon dry mustard
1 tablespoon Worcestershire sauce
1 tablespoon canola oil
2 garlic cloves, minced
Salt and pepper to taste

Barbecue Sauce
1 cup ketchup
1/4 cup minced yellow onion
1/4 cup chicken broth

Rib-Eye Steaks
6 rib-eye steaks
Salt and pepper to taste

To prepare the rub, mix the chili powder, cumin, coriander, dry mustard, oregano and cayenne pepper in a small bowl.

To prepare the sauce, bring the ketchup, onion, broth, vinegar, brown sugar, dry mustard, Worcestershire sauce, canola oil, garlic, salt and pepper to a boil in a medium saucepan. Reduce the heat to low and simmer for 15 minutes, stirring occasionally. Strain the sauce into a bowl; discard the solids.

To prepare the steaks, season each steak with salt and pepper and rub with the dry rub. Grill the steaks over hot coals to the desired degree of doneness. Serve with the barbecue sauce.
Serves 6

Grilled Flank Steak with Caribbean Rice

Flank Steak
1/4 cup vegetable oil
1/4 cup soy sauce
1/4 cup pineapple juice
2 tablespoons brown sugar
2 tablespoons lime juice
2 tablespoons chopped fresh cilantro
2 garlic cloves, chopped
1 tablespoon honey
2 teaspoons ground ginger
1 teaspoon dried crushed red pepper
1 (2-pound) beef flank steak

Caribbean Rice
1 tablespoon olive oil
1/4 cup finely chopped yellow onion
1 garlic clove, minced
1 cup basmati rice
1 1/4 cups water
1/2 cup chicken broth
1/4 cup unsweetened coconut milk
1/2 cup canned yellow corn
1 tablespoon chopped fresh parsley
1 teaspoon grated lime zest
1/2 teaspoon salt

To prepare the steak, mix the oil, soy sauce, pineapple juice, brown sugar, lime juice, cilantro, garlic, honey, ginger and red pepper in a bowl. Pour the soy sauce mixture over the steak in a shallow dish, turning to coat. Marinate, covered, in the refrigerator for 8 to 10 hours, turning occasionally. Drain, reserving the marinade.

Grill the steak over hot coals with the grill lid down for 8 to 10 minutes per side or to the desired degree of doneness, brushing with the reserved marinade as desired. Cease brushing with the marinade 5 minutes before the end of the grilling process, discarding any remaining marinade. Let the steak rest for 7 minutes and cut diagonally across the grain into thin slices.

To prepare the rice, heat the olive oil in a large saucepan over medium-high heat. Sauté the onion and garlic in the hot oil for 1 to 2 minutes or until the onion is tender. Stir in the rice, water, broth and coconut milk and bring to a boil. Reduce the heat to low and simmer, covered, for 25 minutes or until the liquid is absorbed and the rice is tender, stirring occasionally. Stir in the corn, parsley, lime zest and salt. Serve with the steak.
Serves 4

You can also marinate the steak in a sealable plastic bag.

Lasagna

Cottage Cheese Filling
2 cups large curd cottage cheese
1/2 cup (2 ounces) grated
    Parmesan cheese
1 teaspoon parsley flakes
1 teaspoon dried basil
1 teaspoon dried oregano
2 eggs, lightly beaten

Lasagna
1 pound lean ground beef
2 tablespoons olive oil
1 yellow onion, chopped

1 (15-ounce) can tomato sauce
1 (14-ounce) can diced tomatoes
1 (6-ounce) can tomato paste
4 garlic cloves, minced
2 tablespoons dried basil
1 tablespoon dried oregano
1 tablespoon parsley flakes
Salt and pepper to taste
Lasagna noodles, cooked
    and drained
2 (6- to 8-ounce) packages
    mozzarella cheese slices

To prepare the filling, combine the cottage cheese, Parmesan cheese, parsley flakes, basil, oregano and eggs in a bowl and mix well. Store, covered, in the refrigerator.

To prepare the lasagna, brown the ground beef in a skillet, stirring until crumbly; drain. Heat the olive oil in a large saucepan over medium heat and add the onion. Sauté for 6 minutes. Reduce the heat to low and stir in the tomato sauce, tomatoes, tomato paste, garlic, basil, oregano and parsley flakes. Stir in the ground beef. Simmer over low heat for 30 minutes, stirring occasionally. Season with salt and pepper.

Cover the bottom of a lasagna pan with noodles. Layer with half the ground beef mixture, half the cottage cheese mixture and enough mozzarella cheese slices to cover. Top with another layer of noodles, the remaining ground beef mixture and the remaining cottage cheese mixture. Cover with the remaining mozzarella cheese slices. Bake at 350 degrees for 40 to 45 minutes or until the lasagna is heated through and golden brown.
Serves 10 to 12

Cheese and Mushroom Meat Loaf with Buttermilk Mashed Potatoes

Meat Loaf

1 pound lean ground beef
1 cup button mushrooms, thinly sliced
3/4 cup plain bread crumbs
1/2 cup milk
1/4 cup tomato paste
1 egg, lightly beaten
2 tablespoons minced onion
1 tablespoon parsley flakes
1 teaspoon Worcestershire sauce
1/2 teaspoon salt
1/4 teaspoon dry mustard
1/4 teaspoon garlic salt
1/4 teaspoon pepper
1 cup ketchup
1 cup (4 ounces) shredded
    Cheddar cheese

Buttermilk Mashed Potatoes

2 pounds baking potatoes, peeled
    and chopped
1 pound sweet potatoes, peeled
    and chopped
6 cups water
2 tablespoons olive oil
1 teaspoon salt
3/4 cup buttermilk
1/4 cup (1/2 stick) butter
3/4 teaspoon salt
1/2 teaspoon pepper

To prepare the meat loaf, mix the ground beef, mushrooms, bread crumbs, milk, tomato paste, egg and onion in a bowl. Add the parsley flakes, Worcestershire sauce, salt, dry mustard, garlic salt and pepper and mix well. Shape the ground beef mixture into a loaf in a 5×9-inch loaf pan. Bake at 350 degrees for 40 to 45 minutes. Pour the ketchup over the top and bake for 20 to 25 minutes longer or until the meat loaf is no longer pink in the center. Sprinkle with the cheese and bake until the cheese melts. Let stand for 5 minutes before serving.

To prepare the potatoes, combine the baking potatoes, sweet potatoes, water, olive oil and 1 teaspoon salt in a stockpot and bring to a boil. Reduce the heat and cook, covered, for 20 minutes or until the potatoes are tender; drain. Add the buttermilk, butter, 3/4 teaspoon salt and the pepper to the potatoes and mash with a large fork until the desired consistency. Serve with the meat loaf.
Serves 4

Spaghetti and Bolognese Sauce

1 pound ground beef
2 tablespoons olive oil
1/4 cup finely chopped yellow onion
1/4 cup finely chopped carrots
1/4 cup finely chopped celery
2 garlic cloves, minced
3/4 cup milk
Ground nutmeg to taste
1 cup canned diced tomato
1 cup vegetable broth
Salt and pepper to taste
Hot cooked spaghetti
Grated Parmesan cheese to taste

Brown the ground beef in a skillet, stirring until crumbly; drain. Heat the olive oil
in a medium saucepan over medium-high heat and add the onion, carrots and celery.
Cook for 5 minutes, stirring frequently. Stir in the garlic and cook for 1 minute
longer. Add the milk and nutmeg and cook over medium heat until the milk is reduced
by half, stirring frequently.

Add the ground beef, tomato and broth to the milk mixture and simmer for
20 minutes. Season with salt and pepper. Toss the ground beef sauce with spaghetti
in a large serving bowl and sprinkle with Parmesan cheese.
Serves 6 to 8

Molasses-Glazed Pork Roast with Black Pepper Dumplings

Pork Roast
1 (3-pound) boneless pork loin
  roast, trimmed
1 tablespoon olive oil
Salt and pepper to taste
1 cup orange marmalade
1/4 cup molasses
1/4 cup brewed dark coffee
2 tablespoons brown mustard
1 tablespoon vanilla extract

**Black Pepper Dumplings
and Assembly**
8 cups chicken broth
4 cups all-purpose flour
1/4 cup coarsely ground black pepper
1/4 cup chopped fresh parsley
2 tablespoons baking powder
4 teaspoons kosher salt
4 teaspoons chopped fresh thyme
1/2 cup (1 stick) unsalted butter, chilled
1 1/3 cups milk

To prepare the pork, rub the surface of the pork with the olive oil and season with salt and pepper. Arrange the pork on a rack in a foil-lined roasting pan. Roast, covered, at 450 degrees for 45 minutes.

Combine the marmalade, molasses, coffee, brown mustard and vanilla in a medium bowl and mix well. Brush the pork evenly with 1/2 cup of the molasses mixture. Bake for 8 minutes longer or until a meat thermometer inserted in the thickest portion registers 155 degrees. Remove the pork from the oven and pour the remaining molasses mixture over top. Let rest for 15 minutes before slicing, reserving the pan drippings.

To prepare the dumplings, bring the broth to a simmer in a large saucepan. Mix the flour, pepper, parsley, baking powder, salt and thyme in a bowl. Cut the butter into the flour mixture until the mixture resembles coarse cornmeal. Add the milk and stir just until moistened. Shape the dough into a ball and knead several times. Flatten the dough into a disc on a lightly floured surface and cut into twenty-four equal strips.

Drop the dumplings in batches into the simmering broth and cook for 20 minutes or just until the dumplings are puffed and cooked through. Arrange the sliced pork over the dumplings on a serving platter and drizzle with the reserved pan drippings. Garnish with peach slices and sprigs of rosemary.
Serves 8

Roasted Pork Loin with Raspberry Chipotle Glaze

Raspberry Chipotle Glaze

1 tablespoon olive oil
1/2 cup minced yellow onion
1/2 cup raspberry preserves
1/4 cup white vinegar
2 teaspoons minced garlic
2 teaspoons minced seeded
   chipotle chile
1/2 teaspoon salt

Pork Loin

1 (3-pound) boneless pork
   loin, trimmed
Salt and pepper to taste
3 tablespoons olive oil
4 garlic cloves, minced
1 tablespoon minced fresh rosemary
1 tablespoon minced fresh sage
1 tablespoon minced fresh thyme

To prepare the glaze, heat the olive oil in a medium saucepan over medium-high heat and add the onion. Sauté for 4 minutes or until tender and light golden brown. Stir in the preserves, vinegar, garlic, chipotle chile and salt. Bring to a boil and reduce the heat to low. Simmer for 5 minutes, stirring occasionally. Strain into a bowl, discarding the solids. Return the glaze to the saucepan and cover to keep warm.

To prepare the pork, rub the surface of the pork with salt and pepper. Heat the olive oil in a roasting pan. Brown the pork on all sides in the hot oil. Remove the pan from the heat and let stand until the surface of the pork is cool to the touch.

Mix the garlic, rosemary, sage and thyme in a small bowl. Rub the pork with the garlic mixture and roast at 500 degrees until a meat thermometer inserted in the thickest portion registers 155 degrees. Remove the pork to a platter and let rest for 10 minutes. Slice and serve with the raspberry chipotle glaze.

Serves 6

Blackened Pork Chops with Pineapple Mint Chutney and Corn Fritters

Pineapple Mint Chutney
1 cup fresh pineapple chunks
1/4 cup finely chopped red bell pepper
3 tablespoons brown sugar
2 tablespoons white vinegar
2 tablespoons lemon juice
1 tablespoon chopped fresh mint
Salt and pepper to taste

Pork Chops
6 (6-ounce) boneless pork chops
1 cup blackening seasoning
Vegetable oil for searing

Corn Fritters
1/4 cup all-purpose flour
2 pinches of baking powder
2 pinches of salt
2 pinches of pepper
1/4 cup cold water
2 cups yellow corn kernels, puréed
2 eggs, lightly beaten
Vegetable oil for frying

To prepare the chutney, bring the pineapple, bell pepper, brown sugar, vinegar, lemon juice and mint to a boil in a medium saucepan. Reduce the heat to low and simmer for 3 minutes, stirring occasionally. Season with salt and pepper.

To prepare the chops, rub the surface of the chops with the blackening seasoning. Heat a small amount of oil in a skillet until the oil begins to smoke. Add the pork chops to the hot oil and sear each side to blacken. Remove the pork chops to a baking pan and bake at 425 degrees until cooked through.

To prepare the fritters, mix the flour, baking powder, salt and pepper in a bowl. Add the cold water and whisk until blended. Stir in the corn and eggs. Heat enough oil in a deep skillet to cover the fritters. Using a small ice cream scoop, drop the fritter batter into the hot oil and fry until golden brown on both sides; drain. Serve the corn fritters with the pork chops and pineapple mint chutney.
Serves 6

Roasted Pork Chops with Apple Cider Glaze and Mashed Root Vegetables

Apple Cider Glaze

3 cups apple juice
1/2 cup apple cider vinegar
1/2 cup packed brown sugar
1/4 cup honey
2 tablespoons Creole mustard
3 tablespoons unsalted butter, melted
1 teaspoon ground cinnamon
1/4 teaspoon ground allspice
1/4 teaspoon mace
1/4 teaspoon ground cardamom
1/4 cup water
2 tablespoons cornstarch

Mashed Root Vegetables and Assembly

2 quarts (8 cups) water
2 sweet potatoes, peeled and chopped
3 new potatoes, peeled and chopped
1 celery root, peeled and chopped
1 turnip, peeled and chopped
1/2 cup sour cream
1/3 cup unsalted butter, softened
1 tablespoon chopped fresh thyme
Salt and pepper to taste

Pork Chops

8 (6-ounce) pork chops
Salt and pepper to taste
2 tablespoons olive oil

To prepare the glaze, whisk the apple juice, vinegar, brown sugar, honey, Creole mustard, butter, cinnamon, allspice, mace and cardamom in a medium saucepan. Bring to a simmer over medium heat and simmer for 5 minutes, stirring occasionally. Whisk the water and cornstarch in a small bowl until blended. Whisk into the hot apple juice mixture and bring to a boil. Boil for 1 minute and remove from the heat.

To prepare the pork chops, season the pork chops with salt and pepper. Heat the olive oil in a large skillet over high heat and add the pork chops. Sear until brown on both sides. Remove the pork chops to a shallow baking dish and cover with the glaze. Roast at 350 degrees for 15 minutes. Remove from the oven and cover to keep warm.

To prepare the vegetables, bring the water to a boil in a large saucepan and add the sweet potatoes, new potatoes, celery root and turnip. Boil until the vegetables are tender; drain. Whip the potato mixture, sour cream, butter and thyme in a mixing bowl. Season with salt and pepper. Divide the mashed vegetable mixture evenly among eight serving plates. Top each serving with one pork chop and drizzle with the pork chop pan drippings.

Serves 8

Pancetta-Wrapped Pork Chops with Tomato-Mustard Seed Chutney and Dijon Mashed Potatoes

Tomato-Mustard Seed Chutney
1/2 cup packed brown sugar
1/2 cup rice wine vinegar
4 tomatoes, seeded and finely chopped
1/4 cup finely chopped purple onion
1 tablespoon minced fresh ginger
1 tablespoon mustard seeds
Salt and pepper to taste

Dijon Mashed Potatoes
4 russet potatoes, peeled and
    cut into quarters
Salt to taste

3/4 cup sour cream
1/4 cup Dijon mustard
1/3 cup unsalted butter, softened
Pepper to taste

Pork Chops and Assembly
6 (6-ounce) pork chops
Salt and pepper to taste
12 paper-thin slices pancetta
6 leaves radicchio

To prepare the chutney, heat a heavy saucepan over medium heat until hot and then add the brown sugar. Cook until the brown sugar melts and then stir in the vinegar. Cook until the vinegar is incorporated, stirring frequently. Add the tomatoes, onion, ginger and mustard seeds and mix well. Cook over low heat until almost all of the liquid is absorbed, stirring occasionally. Season with salt and pepper.

To prepare the potatoes, combine the potatoes and salt with enough water to cover in a saucepan and bring to a boil. Boil until the potatoes are tender; drain. Mash the potatoes, sour cream, Dijon mustard and butter in a mixing bowl. Season with salt and pepper. Return the mashed potatoes to the saucepan and cover to keep warm.

To prepare the pork chops, season the pork chops lightly with salt and pepper. Wrap each pork chop tightly with 2 slices of the pancetta. Grill over hot coals until cooked through. Place one radicchio leaf in the center of each of six serving plates and top with equal portions of the Dijon mashed potatoes. Arrange the pork chops on the plate in front of the potatoes and spoon the tomato-mustard seed chutney over the pork chops. Serve immediately.
Serves 6

Coconut Chicken with African Spices and Couscous

Chicken

1 tablespoon olive oil
5 boneless skinless
 chicken breasts, chopped
1 yellow onion, finely chopped
2 red bell peppers, finely chopped
1 carrot, finely chopped
1 teaspoon curry powder
1 teaspoon brown sugar
1/2 teaspoon ground ginger
1 cup canned diced tomatoes
1 cup coconut milk
1 cup chicken broth
2 garlic cloves, minced

1 tablespoon grated lemon zest
2 whole cloves
1 golden potato, peeled and chopped
1 sweet potato, peeled and chopped

Couscous and Assembly

2/3 cup olive oil
2 cups couscous
1/2 cup golden raisins
1/2 cup chick-peas
1/4 cup pine nuts, toasted
3 cups chicken broth
Salt and pepper to taste

To prepare the chicken, heat the olive oil in a large stockpot over medium heat. Add the chicken, onion, bell peppers, carrot, curry powder, brown sugar and ginger to the hot oil and sauté for 5 to 7 minutes, until the vegetables are tender. Stir in the tomatoes, coconut milk, broth, garlic, lemon zest and cloves. Bring to a boil and reduce the heat. Stir in the potatoes and simmer for 30 minutes or until the potatoes are tender and the chicken is cooked through, stirring occasionally. Discard the cloves.

To prepare the couscous, combine olive oil, couscous, raisins, chick-peas and pine nuts in a heatproof bowl and mix well. Bring the broth to a boil in a saucepan and pour over the couscous mixture, mixing well. Let stand, covered with plastic wrap, for about 15 minutes. Season with salt and pepper and fluff with a fork. Ladle the coconut chicken over the couscous on a serving platter. Serve immediately.
Serves 5 to 6

This dish placed second in the Best Entrée category at the 2003 Taste of Savannah.

Sautéed Chicken with Harissa Sauce and Couscous

Harissa Sauce
1/4 cup olive oil
3 roasted red peppers
2 small red chiles, seeded and minced
5 garlic cloves, minced
3 tablespoons fresh cilantro, minced
1 tablespoon ground coriander
1 tablespoon lime juice
1 teaspoon ground cumin
1/2 teaspoon ground cardamom
Salt and black pepper to taste

Chicken
4 boneless skinless chicken breasts,
    trimmed and coarsely chopped
1 teaspoon ground cumin

1 teaspoon ground cardamom
Salt and pepper to taste
1 tablespoon olive oil
1 zucchini, cut into 1/4-inch slices
1 cup chicken broth
11/2 cups canned chick-peas, drained
    and rinsed
1 cup canned diced tomatoes with juice
1/2 cup fresh mint, chopped

Couscous and Assembly
2/3 cup olive oil
2 cups couscous
1/2 cup golden raisins
3 cups chicken broth
Salt and pepper to taste

To prepare the sauce, process the olive oil, red peppers, red chiles, garlic, cilantro, coriander, lime juice, cumin and cardamom in a food processor or blender until smooth. Season with salt and black pepper.

To prepare the chicken, toss the chicken with the cumin, cardamom, salt and pepper in bowl until coated. Heat the olive oil in a large skillet over high heat. Sauté the chicken and zucchini in the hot oil until golden brown. Stir in 1/2 cup of the harissa sauce, the broth, chick-peas, tomatoes and mint. Cook just until heated through and season with salt and pepper.

To prepare the couscous, mix the olive oil, couscous, raisins and 1/4 cup of the harissa sauce in a large heatproof bowl. Bring the broth to a boil in a saucepan and pour over the couscous mixture. Stir and let stand, covered with plastic wrap, for 15 minutes. Season with salt and pepper. Divide the couscous evenly among four to six plates and top with the chicken.
Serves 4 to 6

Chicken Piccata with Parmesan-Herb Polenta and Wilted Spinach

Parmesan-Herb Polenta
2 tablespoons olive oil
1/4 cup minced yellow onion
1 garlic clove, minced
1 quart (4 cups) chicken broth
3/4 cup cornmeal (polenta)
1/4 cup (1 ounce) grated
    Parmesan cheese
1 tablespoon minced chives
1 tablespoon minced fresh parsley
Salt and pepper to taste

Chicken Piccata
6 boneless skinless chicken breasts
Salt and black pepper to taste
1 cup all-purpose flour
1 teaspoon garlic powder

Pinch of cayenne pepper
Olive oil for sautéing
6 tablespoons butter
1/4 cup each minced yellow onion, dry
    white wine and lemon juice
1 1/2 cups chicken broth
1/4 cup drained capers
2 tablespoons chopped fresh parsley

Wilted Spinach and Assembly
6 slices bacon, chopped
2 tablespoons butter
1 tablespoon minced yellow onion
1 garlic clove, minced
2 tablespoons red wine vinegar
1 pound fresh spinach, trimmed
Salt and pepper to taste

To prepare the polenta, heat the olive oil in a large saucepan over medium heat and add the onion. Sauté for 2 minutes and then stir in the garlic. Sauté for 1 minute longer. Add the broth and bring to a boil. Gradually add the cornmeal, stirring constantly. Simmer for 10 minutes, stirring constantly. Remove from the heat and stir in the cheese, chives and parsley. Season with salt and pepper. Cover to keep warm.

To prepare the chicken piccata, flatten the chicken breasts between sheets of waxed paper with a meat mallet. Season with salt and black pepper. Mix the flour, garlic powder and cayenne pepper in a dish and coat the chicken with the flour mixture.

    Lightly coat the bottom of a large skillet with olive oil and heat over medium-high heat. Add the chicken and sauté until cooked through and golden brown. Remove the chicken to a platter and cover to keep warm, reserving the pan drippings. Heat the butter with the reserved pan drippings. Add the onion, wine and lemon juice and cook for 3 minutes. Stir in the broth and bring to a simmer. Simmer for 10 minutes and remove from the heat. Stir in the capers and parsley. Cover to keep warm.

To prepare the spinach, combine the bacon, butter and onion in a large skillet over medium heat. Cook for 3 minutes and then stir in the garlic. Cook for 2 minutes and then stir in the vinegar. Cook for 1 minute. Add the spinach one handful at a time, cooking just until wilted. Remove from the heat and season with salt and pepper. Divide the polenta evenly among six plates. Top each serving with equal portions of the spinach and one chicken breast. Drizzle with the caper sauce.

Serves 6

Sautéed Chicken with Cheddar Spinach Grits

Country Ham Sauce
1/4 cup (1/2 stick) unsalted butter
1/4 cup all-purpose flour
1 quart (4 cups) chicken broth
1/4 cup chopped white
    button mushrooms
3 garlic cloves, minced
1 bay leaf
1 teaspoon minced fresh thyme
1 teaspoon minced fresh parsley
8 ounces country ham, finely chopped
1/4 cup milk
2 tablespoons minced fresh sage
Salt and pepper to taste

Cheddar Spinach Grits
6 cups water
1 1/2 cups quick-cooking grits
3 tablespoons unsalted butter
1 teaspoon minced garlic
1 cup (4 ounces) shredded
    Cheddar cheese
2 cups trimmed fresh spinach
    leaves, chopped
Salt and white pepper to taste

Chicken and Assembly
6 boneless skinless
    chicken breasts, trimmed
Salt and pepper to taste
2 tablespoons olive oil

To prepare the sauce, heat the butter in a saucepan until melted. Add the flour and whisk until blended. Cook for 2 minutes over medium heat. Add the broth gradually, whisking constantly. Bring to a boil and then reduce the heat to low. Stir in the mushrooms, garlic, bay leaf, thyme and parsley and simmer for 35 minutes, stirring occasionally. Strain the sauce into a bowl, discarding the solids. Return the sauce to the saucepan and stir in the ham, milk and sage. Simmer just until heated through and season with salt and pepper. Remove from the heat and cover to keep warm.

To prepare the grits, bring the water to a boil in a large heavy saucepan. Add the grits, butter and garlic and mix well. Reduce the heat to low and cook until thick and creamy, stirring occasionally. Remove from the heat and stir in the cheese and spinach. Season with salt and white pepper. Cover to keep warm.

To prepare the chicken, flatten the chicken between sheets of waxed paper with a meat mallet. Season with salt and pepper. Heat the olive oil in a large sauté pan over medium-high heat. Sauté the chicken in the hot oil until golden brown and cooked through. Spoon equal portions of the grits on each of six plates. Top each serving with one chicken breast and drizzle with the country ham sauce.
Serves 6

Thai Chicken with Sweet Chile-Garlic Sauce and Cilantro Lime Rice

Sweet Chile-Garlic Sauce
1 cup sugar
2 cups white vinegar
1 tablespoon crushed red pepper flakes
1 teaspoon minced garlic
Salt to taste

Cilantro Lime Rice
1 tablespoon olive oil
1/4 cup finely chopped yellow onion
1 cup white rice
2 cups water
1 tablespoon lime juice
2 teaspoons grated lime zest
1 bay leaf

1 sprig of thyme
Salt and pepper to taste
2 tablespoons chopped fresh cilantro

Chicken and Assembly
1 1/4 cups coconut milk
1/4 cup chopped fresh cilantro
2 tablespoons soy sauce
2 garlic cloves, minced
1 1/2 teaspoons turmeric
1 1/2 teaspoons sugar
6 boneless skinless chicken breasts,
    trimmed and chopped
Salt and white pepper to taste
Canola oil for sautéing

To prepare the sauce, heat the sugar in a small saucepan over medium heat until the sugar melts and turns golden brown. Whisk in the vinegar until blended. Remove from the heat and stir in the red pepper flakes, garlic and salt. Cover to keep warm.

To prepare the rice, heat the olive oil in a large saucepan over medium heat. Sauté the onion in the hot oil for 2 minutes or until tender. Add the rice and cook for 3 minutes, stirring occasionally. Stir in the water, lime juice, lime zest, bay leaf and thyme. Bring to a boil and reduce the heat to low. Cook, covered, for 20 minutes or until the liquid is absorbed and the rice is tender. Discard the bay leaf and thyme sprig. Season with salt and pepper and stir in the cilantro. Cover to keep warm.

To prepare the chicken, bring the coconut milk, cilantro, soy sauce, garlic, turmeric and sugar to a boil in a large saucepan. Reduce the heat to low and simmer for 15 minutes, stirring occasionally.

Season the chicken with salt and white pepper. Lightly coat a large skillet with canola oil and heat over medium-high heat. Sauté the chicken in the hot oil until golden brown on all sides. Add the chicken to the coconut milk mixture and mix well. Simmer for 15 minutes, stirring occasionally. Season with salt and white pepper if needed. Ladle the chicken over the cilantro lime rice on a serving platter. Serve with the sweet chile-garlic sauce.

Serves 6

Lime Cilantro Chicken with Chili Butter

Chicken

8 boneless skinless chicken breasts
1/2 cup vegetable oil
1/4 cup cider vinegar
1/4 cup lime juice
2 tablespoons orange juice
1 tablespoon chopped fresh cilantro
1 jalapeño chile, seeded and minced
1 teaspoon minced garlic
1 teaspoon chili powder
1 teaspoon ground cumin
Salt and pepper to taste

Chili Butter

1 cup (2 sticks) unsalted
    butter, softened
1 1/2 teaspoons chili powder
1 1/2 teaspoons chopped fresh oregano
1 teaspoon hot red pepper sauce
1 teaspoon Worcestershire sauce
1/2 teaspoon paprika
1/4 teaspoon garlic powder
1/4 teaspoon onion powder
1/4 teaspoon ground cumin
Salt and pepper to taste

To prepare the chicken, flatten the chicken breasts between sheets of waxed paper with a meat mallet. Arrange the chicken in a single layer in a shallow dish. Mix the oil, vinegar, lime juice, orange juice, cilantro, jalapeño chile, garlic, chili powder, cumin, salt and pepper in a bowl and pour over the chicken, turning to coat. Marinate, covered, in the refrigerator for 1 to 10 hours, turning occasionally; drain. Grill the chicken over hot coals until cooked through.

To prepare the chili butter, combine the butter, chili powder, oregano, hot sauce, Worcestershire sauce, paprika, garlic powder, onion powder and cumin in a bowl and mix well. Season with salt and pepper. Top each chicken breast with some of the butter and serve immediately.

Serves 8

This is wonderful served with sliced avocado and orange segments.

Orecchiette with Chicken

1/3 cup extra-virgin olive oil
4 boneless skinless chicken breasts, trimmed and chopped
1 cup sun-dried tomatoes, chopped
1/2 cup finely chopped prosciutto
8 garlic cloves, thinly sliced
1/4 cup pine nuts
1/4 teaspoon red pepper flakes
Salt and black pepper to taste
16 ounces orecchiette
1 cup crumbled gorgonzola cheese

Heat the olive oil in a large sauté pan over medium heat. Add the chicken, tomatoes and prosciutto and sauté until the chicken is golden brown and cooked through. Stir in the garlic, pine nuts and red pepper flakes. Cook for 2 minutes and season with salt and black pepper.

Bring a large saucepan three-fourths full of salted water to a boil over high heat. Stir in the pasta and cook using the package directions until al dente; drain. Toss the hot pasta with the chicken mixture and cheese in a large bowl. Serve in individual pasta bowls.

Serves 6

Crab Meat-Stuffed Flounder

Crab Meat Stuffing
1 tablespoon olive oil
1/2 red bell pepper, finely chopped
1/2 small yellow onion, finely chopped
8 ounces crab meat, drained
   and flaked
4 ounces reduced-fat cream
   cheese, softened
1 tablespoon Dijon mustard
1 tablespoon Worcestershire sauce
1 teaspoon Old Bay seasoning
Salt and pepper to taste

Lemon Basil Sauce
6 tablespoons unsalted butter
1/4 cup minced yellow onion
1/2 cup all-purpose flour
2 cups vegetable broth
Grated zest and juice of 3 lemons
2 tablespoons chopped fresh basil
Salt and pepper to taste

Flounder and Assembly
6 flounder fillets
Salt and pepper to taste
2 tablespoons olive oil
2 cups vegetable broth

To prepare the stuffing, heat the olive oil in a large sauté pan and add the bell pepper and onion. Sauté for 4 to 5 minutes or until the vegetables are tender. Let stand until cool. Combine the bell pepper mixture, crab meat, cream cheese, Dijon mustard, Worcestershire sauce and Old Bay seasoning in a bowl and mix well. Season with salt and pepper.

To prepare the sauce, heat the butter in a large saucepan until melted. Stir in the onion and cook for 2 minutes. Add the flour and whisk until combined. Cook over medium heat for 2 minutes, stirring frequently. Add the broth gradually, whisking constantly until combined. Bring to a boil and reduce the heat. Simmer until of a sauce consistency, stirring frequently. Stir in the lemon zest, lemon juice and basil. Season with salt and pepper. Remove from the heat and cover to keep warm.

To prepare the flounder, season each fillet lightly with salt and pepper. Make a pocket in each fillet and spoon the crab meat stuffing evenly into the pockets. Heat the olive oil in a large sauté pan and add the fillets. Sauté for 2 minutes per side or until golden brown. Remove the fillets to a shallow baking dish and add the broth. Bake at 375 degrees until the fillets are opaque and firm to the touch; the time will depend on the thickness of the fillets. Serve with the lemon basil sauce.
Serves 6

Grilled Salmon with Black Bean Salsa and Chipotle Orange Vinaigrette

Black Bean Salsa
2 cups canned black beans, drained
    and rinsed
1/4 cup finely chopped red bell pepper
1/4 cup finely chopped green
    bell pepper
1/4 cup finely chopped purple onion
1 jalapeño chile, seeded and minced
2 garlic cloves, minced
1 tablespoon chopped fresh cilantro
1/2 teaspoon ground cinnamon
2 tablespoons lime juice
2 tablespoons red wine vinegar
1 tablespoon olive oil
Salt and pepper to taste

Chipotle Orange Vinaigrette
1/2 cup orange juice
2 tablespoons sherry vinegar

1 tablespoon minced fresh cilantro
1 tablespoon minced fresh oregano
2 teaspoons honey
1 teaspoon minced chipotle chile in
    adobe sauce (see note below)
1 teaspoon grated lime zest
1/2 teaspoon chili powder
1/2 teaspoon ground cumin
1/3 cup canola oil
Salt and pepper to taste

Salmon and Assembly
6 (6-ounce) skinless salmon fillets
Salt and pepper to taste
Olive oil for coating

To prepare the salsa, combine the beans, bell peppers, onion, jalapeño chile, garlic, cilantro and cinnamon in a bowl and mix well. Stir in the lime juice, vinegar and olive oil. Season with salt and pepper.

To prepare the vinaigrette, mix the orange juice, vinegar, cilantro, oregano, honey and chipotle chile in a bowl. Stir in the lime zest, chili powder and cumin. Gradually add the canola oil, whisking constantly until incorporated. Season with salt and pepper.

To prepare the salmon, season the fillets with salt and pepper and rub with olive oil. Grill over hot coals until the fillets flake easily; the time will depend on the thickness of the fillets. Arrange the fillets on each of six plates and drizzle with the vinaigrette. Garnish with sprigs of cilantro and serve with the salsa.
Serves 6

If using dried chipotle chiles, rehydrate in hot water for 20 minutes. Drain, finely chop and combine with a little olive oil and vinegar.

Poached Salmon with Lemon Butter Sauce and Sour Cream-Dill Mashed Potatoes

Salmon
2 quarts (8 cups) vegetable broth
1 lemon, sliced
1 tablespoon Old Bay seasoning
1 bay leaf
6 (6-ounce) salmon fillets
Salt and pepper to taste

Lemon Butter Sauce
2 tablespoons minced green onions
6 tablespoons butter, chilled and cubed
2 tomatoes, seeded and chopped
2 tablespoons lemon juice

1 tablespoon chopped fresh dill weed
Salt and freshly ground pepper to taste

**Sour Cream-Dill Mashed Potatoes
and Assembly**
2 pounds red potatoes, cut into quarters
Salt to taste
1 cup sour cream
1/2 cup heavy cream
1/4 cup (1/2 stick) unsalted butter
1 tablespoon chopped fresh dill weed
Pepper to taste

To prepare the salmon, combine the broth, lemon, Old Bay seasoning and bay leaf in a large stockpot and bring to a low simmer. Season the fillets with salt and pepper and arrange in the poaching liquid; the fillets must be covered by the liquid. Simmer until the fillets are opaque and firm to the touch; the cooking time will depend on the thickness of the fillets. Remove from the heat, leaving the fillets submerged in the liquid.

To prepare the sauce, strain 1/2 cup of the poaching liquid, discarding the solids. Pour the strained liquid into a large skillet and add the green onions. Bring to a boil and boil until the liquid is reduced by half. Remove from the heat and whisk in the butter. Stir in the tomatoes, lemon juice and dill weed. Season with salt and pepper.

To prepare the potatoes, combine the potatoes with enough salted water to cover in a large saucepan and bring to a boil. Boil until very tender; drain. Beat the potatoes in a mixing bowl at low speed just until broken up. Add the sour cream, heavy cream, butter and dill weed and beat until the desired consistency. Season with salt and pepper. Divide the mashed potatoes evenly among six plates. Drain the salmon, discarding the liquid. Top each serving with one salmon fillet and drizzle with the lemon butter sauce. Serve immediately.
Serves 6

Substitute sea bass or halibut for the salmon if desired.

Red Snapper Tacos

Grated zest and juice of 2 limes
1/4 cup olive oil
2 tablespoons chili powder
2 tablespoons chopped fresh cilantro
1 tablespoon ground coriander
2 teaspoons ground cumin
1/2 teaspoon ground red pepper
6 (6-ounce) red snapper fillets
6 flour or corn tortillas, heated
11/2 cups shredded iceberg lettuce
1 cup (4 ounces) shredded Pepper Jack cheese
1 cup sour cream
1 cup chopped seeded tomato
1 ripe avocado, chopped
6 lime wedges

Combine the lime zest, lime juice, olive oil, chili powder, cilantro, coriander, cumin and red pepper in a bowl and mix well. Pour the lime juice mixture over the fillets in a shallow dish, turning to coat. Marinate, covered, in the refrigerator for 1 to 4 hours, turning occasionally; drain. Grill over hot coals until the fillets flake easily.

Layer each tortilla with one fillet and equal portions of the lettuce, cheese, sour cream, tomato and avocado. Squeeze the juice from 1 lime wedge over each taco and serve immediately.

Makes 6 tacos

Tilapia Amandine with Creole Meunière Sauce

Creole Seasoning
1 tablespoon paprika
1 tablespoon salt
1 tablespoon garlic powder
1 teaspoon black pepper
1 teaspoon onion powder
1 teaspoon cayenne pepper
1 teaspoon dried oregano
1 teaspoon dried thyme

Tilapia
6 tilapia fillets, skin removed
1 cup milk

2 cups all-purpose flour
1/3 cup olive oil
1 tablespoon butter
1 tablespoon Worcestershire sauce
Juice of 1 lemon
1/2 cup (1 stick) butter, chilled and
  cubed
1 cup pecans, toasted
1 tablespoon chopped fresh parsley
1 tablespoon minced green onions
Grated zest of 1 lemon

To prepare the seasoning, mix the paprika, salt, garlic powder, black pepper, onion powder, cayenne pepper, oregano and thyme in a bowl.

To prepare the tilapia, sprinkle the fillets with the desired amount of the Creole seasoning and arrange in a single layer in a shallow dish. Pour the milk over the fillets and chill, covered, for 1 hour; drain.

Mix the flour and remaining Creole seasoning in a shallow dish. Coat the fillets with the flour mixture. Heat a portion of the olive oil and a portion of 1 tablespoon butter in a sauté pan over medium-high heat. Fry the fillets in the hot oil mixture in batches until golden brown on both sides and cooked through, adding the remaining olive oil and remaining 1 tablespoon butter as needed. Drain the fillets of any excess oil mixture. Keep the fillets warm on a baking sheet in a 200-degree oven.

Strain the oil mixture, reserving the browned bits. Mix the Worcestershire sauce and lemon juice with the browned bits in the sauté pan. Cook for 3 to 4 minutes to allow the liquid to reduce. Reduce the heat to low. Add 1/2 cup butter one cube at a time, whisking constantly until incorporated. Cook until of a sauce consistency and stir in the pecans, parsley, green onions and lemon zest. Drizzle over the fillets and serve immediately.
Serves 6

A mixture of olive oil and butter are used as the frying medium for this dish. The reason is to give the fillets a nice rich butter flavor, while the olive oil prevents the butter from burning over the high heat.

Blackened Tuna and Roasted Vegetable Salsa with Smoked Corn Sauce

Roasted Vegetable Salsa
2 large tomatoes
1 large red onion
1 large red bell pepper
1 jalapeño chile
1 tablespoon lime juice
1 teaspoon minced garlic
1/2 teaspoon hot red pepper sauce
1/4 teaspoon ground cumin
Salt and pepper to taste

Smoked Corn Sauce
6 ears of corn, husks and silk
   removed
3 tablespoons unsalted butter

1/4 cup minced yellow onion
1 cup milk
1 teaspoon salt
1 bay leaf
1/4 teaspoon white pepper
1/4 teaspoon minced garlic
1/4 teaspoon minced fresh sage
1/4 teaspoon ground cumin
Pinch of cayenne pepper

Tuna
4 (6-ounce) tuna steaks
Blackening seasoning to taste
1/4 cup olive oil
2 tablespoons unsalted butter

To prepare the salsa, arrange the tomatoes, onion, bell pepper and jalapeño chile on a grill rack over hot coals. Grill until the vegetables are charred on all sides, turning frequently. Remove the vegetables to a large bowl and cover with plastic wrap. Let stand until cool. Peel, seed and finely chop the vegetables and jalapeño chile. Mix with the lime juice, garlic, hot sauce and cumin in a bowl. Season with salt and pepper.

To prepare the sauce, sprinkle 2 cups presoaked hickory chips over medium-hot coals. Smoke the ears of corn over the hot coals in a covered grill for 20 to 30 minutes until the corn is golden brown, turning several times. Let stand until cool and then cut the kernels into a bowl, discarding the cobs.

Melt the butter in a medium saucepan over medium-high heat. Add the corn and onion and cook for 3 minutes or until the onion is tender. Stir in the milk, salt, bay leaf, white pepper, garlic, sage, cumin and cayenne pepper. Simmer for 25 minutes. Remove from the heat and discard the bay leaf. Process the sauce in a blender or food processor until puréed. Return the sauce to the saucepan and heat just until warm. Remove from the heat and cover to keep warm.

To prepare the tuna, coat the steaks with blackening seasoning. Heat the olive oil and butter in a large cast-iron skillet over medium-high heat until the butter melts. Cook the tuna in the butter mixture for 2 minutes per side or to the desired degree of donenesss. Serve with the roasted vegetable salsa and smoked corn sauce.
Serves 4

Grilled Tuna with Pecan Lime Butter

Tuna
5 (5-ounce) tuna steaks
Salt and pepper to taste
1/2 cup canola oil
1/4 cup white wine vinegar
1 tablespoon chopped fresh cilantro
1 tablespoon lemon juice
1 green onion, minced
1 teaspoon minced garlic
Pinch of nutmeg

Pecan Lime Butter
1/2 cup (1 stick) unsalted butter,
    softened
1 tablespoon pecan pieces, toasted and
    finely crushed
1 tablespoon lime juice
1 tablespoon minced fresh cilantro
1 teaspoon minced garlic
Salt and pepper to taste

To prepare the tuna, season the steaks with salt and pepper and arrange in a shallow dish. Combine the canola oil, vinegar, cilantro, lemon juice, green onion, garlic and nutmeg in a bowl and mix well. Pour the marinade over the steaks, turning to coat. Marinate, covered, in the refrigerator for 1 to 2 hours, turning occasionally. Grill for 2 to 3 minutes per side or to the desired degree of doneness.

To prepare the pecan lime butter, mix the butter, pecans, lime juice, cilantro and garlic in a bowl. Season with salt and pepper. Serve a pat of the pecan lime butter with each steak. Garnish with lemon wedges and sprigs of cilantro.
Serves 5

Crispy Crab Cakes with Mango and Green Onion Relish

Mango and Green Onion Relish
2 large mangoes, chopped
1/2 red onion, finely chopped
2 green onions, minced
1 jalapeño chile, seeded and minced
2 tablespoons finely chopped
    red bell pepper
1 tablespoon chopped fresh cilantro
2 tablespoons lime juice
2 tablespoons olive oil
Salt and pepper to taste

Crab Cakes
8 ounces lump crab meat, drained
8 ounces claw crab meat, drained
1/2 cup panko
2 tablespoons minced red bell pepper
1 tablespoon minced green onion
1 egg, lightly beaten
3 tablespoons cream cheese, softened
2 tablespoons Dijon mustard
1 tablespoon prepared horseradish
1 teaspoon Old Bay seasoning
Olive oil for sautéing

To prepare the relish, combine the mangoes, red onion, green onions, jalapeño chile, bell pepper and cilantro in a bowl and mix well. Stir in the lime juice and olive oil and season with salt and pepper. Chill, covered, for 1 to 10 hours.

To prepare the crab cakes, gently mix the crab meat, bread crumbs, bell pepper and green onion in a bowl. Add the egg, cream cheese, Dijon mustard, horseradish and Old Bay seasoning and mix well. Shape the crab meat mixture into twelve patties.

Heat a small amount of olive oil in a large skillet over medium-high heat. Sauté the crab cakes in the hot oil for 3 minutes per side or until light brown and crisp; drain. Serve with the mango and green onion relish.
Serves 6

Fettuccini with Sea Scallops

1/4 cup olive oil
1 yellow onion, finely chopped
1 (28-ounce) can diced tomatoes
2 cups green peas
1/2 cup canned artichoke hearts, drained and chopped
1/2 cup crumbled goat cheese
3 garlic cloves, minced
6 fresh basil leaves, chopped
2 tablespoons olive oil
18 sea scallops
Salt and freshly ground pepper to taste
16 ounces fettuccini, cooked and drained

Heat 1/4 cup olive oil in a saucepan over medium heat until hot but not smoking.
Add the onion to the hot oil and cook for 5 to 6 minutes or until the onion is tender.
Stir in the tomatoes, peas, artichokes, cheese, garlic and basil. Bring to a simmer
and reduce the heat to medium-low. Cook for 10 to 12 minutes, stirring occasionally.

Heat 2 tablespoons olive oil in a medium sauté pan over medium-high heat
until smoking. Arrange the scallops in an even layer in the hot oil and allow them
to caramelize and cook for 2 minutes per side. Remove from the heat.

Season the tomato sauce with salt and pepper and toss with the pasta in a large
bowl until coated. Divide the pasta mixture evenly among six bowls. Top each
serving with three scallops and serve immediately.
Serves 6

The sea scallops are cooked last and separately from the sauce ingredients because they
can easily overcook, causing them to be rubbery.

Variation: Omitting the sea scallops turns this into a wonderful vegetarian pasta dish.
You can also substitute three chicken breasts for the sea scallops for a less expensive
alternative.

Shrimp and Artichokes over Parmesan Grits

5 cups chicken broth
$1/2$ cup half-and-half
1 tablespoon butter
$1^1/4$ cups instant grits
1 cup (4 ounces) grated Parmesan cheese
Salt and pepper to taste
1 pound medium shrimp, peeled and deveined
1 tablespoon olive oil
1 cup canned artichokes, drained
2 tablespoons minced yellow onion
1 tablespoon lemon juice
3 garlic cloves, minced
1 tablespoon minced fresh oregano

Bring the broth, half-and-half and butter to a boil in a medium saucepan. Add the grits gradually, stirring constantly. Reduce the heat to low and cook until thick and creamy, stirring occasionally. Remove from the heat and stir in the cheese. Season with salt and pepper. Cover to keep warm.

Season the shrimp with salt and pepper. Heat the olive oil in a large sauté pan over high heat. Add the shrimp, artichokes, onion and lemon juice. Sauté until the shrimp turn pink. Stir in the garlic and oregano. Cook for 1 minute, stirring frequently. Divide the grits evenly among four plates. Spoon the shrimp mixture evenly over the grits.
Serves 4

Panko-Fried Shrimp with Orange Chipotle Hollandaise Sauce and Lemon Orange Rice

Essence
5 tablespoons paprika
1/4 cup salt
1/4 cup garlic powder
2 tablespoons black pepper
2 tablespoons onion powder
2 tablespoons cayenne pepper
2 tablespoons oregano
2 tablespoons thyme

Orange Chipotle Hollandaise Sauce
1/2 cup orange juice
2 tablespoons minced yellow onion
8 egg yolks
2 cups (4 sticks) butter, melted
1 tablespoon lemon juice
2 teaspoons puréed seeded
    chipotle chiles
Salt and pepper to taste

Lemon Orange Rice
1/4 cup finely chopped yellow onion
1 tablespoon olive oil
1 cup white rice
2 cups water
1 1/2 teaspoons lemon juice
1 1/2 teaspoons orange juice
1 teaspoon grated lemon zest
1 teaspoon grated orange zest
1 bay leaf
1 sprig of thyme
Salt and pepper to taste

Shrimp and Assembly
2 cups all-purpose flour
4 eggs
1/4 cup milk
1 pound medium shrimp, peeled
3 cups panko

To prepare the essence, mix all the ingredients in a bowl.

To prepare the sauce, boil the orange juice and onion in a saucepan until reduced by half. Let stand until cool. Whisk in the egg yolks. Cook in a double boiler over simmering water until thickened, whisking constantly. Gradually add the butter, whisking constantly until incorporated. Remove from the heat and stir in the lemon juice and chipotle purée. Season with salt and pepper.

To prepare the rice, sauté the onion in the olive oil in a saucepan until tender and then stir in the rice. Cook for 3 minutes. Stir in the water, lemon juice, orange juice, lemon zest, orange zest, bay leaf and thyme. Bring to a boil and reduce the heat to low. Cook, covered, for 20 minutes or until the rice is tender. Discard the bay leaf and thyme; season with salt and pepper. Cover to keep warm.

To prepare the shrimp, mix the flour and essence in a shallow dish. Whisk the eggs and milk in a bowl until blended. Coat the shrimp with the flour mixture, shaking off any excess. Dip in the egg mixture and then coat with the bread crumbs. Heat enough oil in a large deep skillet to cover the shrimp. Fry the shrimp in hot oil until golden brown on all sides and cooked through; drain. Divide the rice and shrimp evenly among four plates. Drizzle with the orange chipotle hollandaise sauce.

Serves 4

Low-Country Boil with Lemon Butter and Cocktail Sauce

Low-Country Boil Seasoning
2 tablespoons mustard seeds
2 tablespoons salt
1 tablespoon black peppercorns
1 tablespoon crushed red pepper flakes
1 tablespoon celery leaves
1 tablespoon coriander seeds
3 bay leaves
1 teaspoon ground ginger

Lemon Butter
1/2 cup (1 stick) butter, softened
Grated zest of 2 lemons

Cocktail Sauce
2 cups ketchup
6 tablespoons prepared horseradish
1/4 cup grated onion
3 tablespoons fresh lemon juice
1 tablespoon Worcestershire sauce

Low-Country Boil
12 red new potatoes, cut into quarters
4 links andouille, cut into 2-inch pieces
3 ears of sweet corn, cut into thirds
Lemons, cut into halves
36 unpeeled shrimp

To prepare the seasoning, process all the ingredients in a blender or coffee grinder until finely ground. To use, allow 2 teaspoons plus 1/2 lemon per quart of water.

To prepare the lemon butter, mix the butter and lemon zest in a bowl.

To prepare the cocktail sauce, mix the ketchup, horseradish, onion, lemon juice and Worcestershire sauce in a bowl. Chill, covered, in the refrigerator.

To prepare the low-country boil, combine the potatoes, sausage and corn in a large stockpot. Add enough water to cover the potato mixture. Stir in the designated amount of low-boil seasoning and lemons per the instructions above. Cook for 15 minutes or until the potatoes are tender. Add the shrimp and cook just until the shrimp turn pink; drain. Serve with the lemon butter and cocktail sauce.
Serves 8

Louisiana-Style Barbecued Shrimp with Corn Maque Choux

Corn Maque Choux

2 tablespoons olive oil
1 link andouille, finely chopped
4 cups sweet corn kernels
1/2 cup finely chopped green bell pepper
2 tablespoons finely chopped onion
1/2 cup canned diced tomatoes
1/2 cup heavy cream
Pinch of cayenne pepper
Salt and black pepper to taste

Shrimp and Assembly

1 tablespoon olive oil
1/4 cup minced yellow onion

1 cup vegetable broth
1 cup clam juice
1 cup heavy cream
2 garlic cloves, minced
3 tablespoons Worcestershire sauce
Juice of 1 lemon
1 tablespoon Creole seasoning
1 bay leaf
Salt and pepper to taste
31 medium shrimp
4 to 6 buttermilk biscuits, baked and
    split into halves

To prepare the maque choux, heat the olive oil in a large saucepan over medium heat and add the sausage. Sauté for 2 to 3 minutes. Stir in the corn, bell pepper and onion and sauté for 7 minutes. Add the tomatoes, cream and cayenne pepper and mix well. Simmer for 15 minutes, stirring occasionally. Season with salt and black pepper. Remove from the heat and cover to keep warm.

To prepare the shrimp, heat the olive oil in a large saucepan over high heat. Sauté the onion in the hot oil for 1 minute. Reduce the heat to medium and stir in the broth, clam juice, cream, garlic, Worcestershire sauce, lemon juice, Creole seasoning and bay leaf. Bring to a simmer and cook for 30 minutes, stirring occasionally. Remove from the heat and strain into a heatproof bowl, discarding the solids. Return the strained sauce to the saucepan and season with salt and pepper. Bring to a simmer and mix in the shrimp. Cook just until the shrimp turn pink. Arrange two biscuit halves on each of four to six plates and spoon the shrimp and sauce over the biscuits. Serve immediately with the corn maque choux.

Serves 4 to 6

Seafood Stew

1/4 cup olive oil
2 tablespoons unsalted butter
1 yellow onion, finely chopped
2 ribs celery, finely chopped
2 leek bulbs, thinly sliced
2 carrots, finely chopped
5 garlic cloves, minced
1/2 cup dry white wine
1 quart (4 cups) vegetable broth
2 cups tomato juice
4 plum tomatoes, finely chopped
1 teaspoon saffron
Grated zest and juice of 2 lemons
1 pound mussels, scrubbed
1 pound littleneck clams, scrubbed
1 pound halibut, cut into large pieces
8 ounces scallops
8 large shrimp, peeled and deveined
Salt and pepper to taste
1/4 cup chopped Italian parsley

Heat the olive oil and butter in a large stockpot over medium heat. Add the onion, celery, leeks and carrots to the butter mixture and cook for 7 minutes, stirring frequently. Stir in the garlic and cook for 1 minute. Stir in the wine, broth, tomato juice and tomatoes.

Bring to a simmer and then stir in the saffron, lemon zest and lemon juice. Simmer for 20 minutes, stirring occasionally. Add the mussels and clams and bring to a boil. Reduce the heat to low and add the halibut, scallops and shrimp. Simmer for 4 minutes and season with salt and pepper. Ladle the stew into bowls and sprinkle with the parsley. Serve immediately with crusty bread.
Serves 4

Photograph for this recipe is shown on page 65.

Curried Broccoli

1 head broccoli, trimmed and cut into
    bite-size pieces
3 tablespoons unsalted butter, softened
1/4 cup golden raisins

1 tablespoon olive oil
1 teaspoon lemon juice
1 teaspoon curry powder
Salt and pepper to taste

Fill a stockpot three-fourths full of water and bring to a boil over high heat. Add the broccoli to the boiling water and cook for 3 minutes or just until the broccoli is tender; drain. Rinse with cold water to cool.

Melt the butter in a large skillet and add the raisins, olive oil, lemon juice and curry powder. Stir in the broccoli and sauté just until the broccoli is heated through. Season with salt and pepper.

Serves 4 to 6

Braised Red Cabbage

2 tablespoons unsalted butter
1 small red onion, thinly sliced
1/2 head red cabbage, thinly sliced
1 green apple, peeled and thinly sliced

Salt and pepper to taste
1/2 cup apple cider
1/4 cup red wine vinegar
2 cinnamon sticks

Melt the butter in a large skillet over medium heat and add the onion, cabbage and apple. Sauté for 5 minutes and season with salt and pepper. Stir in the cider, vinegar and cinnamon sticks. Simmer, covered, for 20 minutes. Discard the cinnamon sticks and adjust the seasonings if needed.

Serves 8

You may prepare Braised Red Cabbage up to one day in advance and store, covered, in the refrigerator. Reheat before serving.

Grilled Corn on the Cob with Spiced Butter

Spiced Butter
1/4 cup (1/2 stick) unsalted butter, softened
1 teaspoon grated lemon zest
1 teaspoon brown sugar
1/2 teaspoon ground cinnamon
1/2 teaspoon ground cloves
1/4 teaspoon cayenne pepper

Corn on the Cob
4 ears of white or yellow corn, husks and silk removed
Olive oil to taste
Salt and pepper to taste

To prepare the spiced butter, mix the butter, lemon zest, brown sugar, cinnamon, cloves and cayenne pepper in a bowl.

To prepare the corn, rub the ears with olive oil and season with salt and pepper. Grill over hot coals to the desired degree of crispness. Serve with the spiced butter.
Serves 4

Steamed Green Beans with Blistered Tomatoes

1 cup water
1 pound fresh green beans, trimmed
1 tablespoon olive oil
1 1/2 cups grape tomatoes
2 tablespoons unsalted butter
Salt and pepper to taste

Bring the water to a boil in a large deep sauté pan. Add the beans to the boiling water and simmer, covered, for 3 minutes; drain. Immediately immerse the beans in a bowl of ice water to stop the cooking process. Let stand until cool; drain.

Heat the olive oil in a large sauté pan over high heat until smoking. Carefully add the tomatoes to the hot oil and sauté just until the tomatoes blister. Reduce the heat to medium and add the beans. Cook for 2 minutes or until the beans are heated through. Stir in the butter and season with salt and pepper.
Serves 6

Roasted Rosemary Red Potatoes

10 red new potatoes, cut into quarters
1/4 cup olive oil
1/4 cup minced garlic
1 1/2 teaspoons dried rosemary
Salt and pepper to taste

Soak the potatoes in a bowl of cool water; drain. Toss the potatoes with the olive oil, garlic and rosemary in a bowl. Season with salt and pepper.

Arrange the potatoes in a single layer on a baking sheet. Roast at 400 degrees for 20 to 25 minutes or until cooked through and golden brown, turning occasionally.
Serves 4 to 6

Acorn Squash Risotto with Spinach and Bacon

1 cup chopped bacon
2 tablespoons olive oil
2 pounds acorn squash, peeled and chopped
1/2 yellow onion, chopped
1 carrot, chopped
6 cups vegetable broth or chicken broth
2 tablespoons minced fresh sage
1 teaspoon minced fresh rosemary
7 tablespoons unsalted butter
2 cups arborio rice
1/2 cup dry white wine
2 cups fresh spinach, chopped
1/2 cup (2 ounces) grated Parmigiano-Reggiano cheese
Salt and freshly ground pepper to taste

Cook the bacon in a skillet until brown and crisp; drain. Heat the olive oil in a large stockpot over medium heat and add the squash, onion and carrot. Sauté for 4 minutes and then stir in the broth, sage and rosemary. Cook for 25 to 30 minutes or until the squash and carrot are tender, stirring occasionally. Purée the squash mixture in batches in a blender or food processor, or use an immersion blender. Return the purée to the stockpot and cover to keep warm.

Melt the butter in a large saucepan over medium heat. Add the rice and cook for about 3 minutes or until the grains are coated and almost translucent, stirring frequently. Add the wine and cook for 5 minutes or until the liquid is absorbed. Add one ladleful of the warm purée and cook just until absorbed, stirring frequently. Add the remaining purée one ladleful at a time, cooking until the purée is absorbed after each addition and stirring frequently. The process should take about 30 minutes. Stir in the bacon, spinach and cheese and season with salt and pepper.

Serves 6

Four-Cheese Risotto

1 large sweet onion, chopped
3 tablespoons olive oil
2 garlic cloves, crushed
1 pound arborio rice
1 cup dry white wine
8 cups chicken broth, heated
1/4 cup (1 ounce) shredded Parmesan cheese
1/4 cup crumbled blue cheese
1/4 cup (1 ounce) shredded smoked Gouda cheese
1/4 cup (1 ounce) shredded Pepper Jack cheese
2 tablespoons butter
1 teaspoon salt

Sweat the onion in the olive oil in a medium saucepan for 3 minutes, stirring constantly. Stir in the garlic and sweat for 2 minutes longer, stirring constantly. Reduce the heat to medium and stir in the rice. Cook for 3 minutes, stirring constantly. Add the wine and cook until the wine is absorbed.

Stir 1 cup of the broth into the rice mixture and cook until the broth is absorbed. Add the remaining broth 1 cup at a time, cooking until the broth is absorbed after each addition. Remove from the heat and stir in the Parmesan cheese, blue cheese, Gouda cheese, Pepper Jack cheese, butter and salt.
Serves 6

To sweat onions, cook until the onions are softened but not brown, stirring constantly and adjusting the heat as needed to prevent browning.

Three Cheese Grits

2 cups water
2/3 cup milk
2/3 cup quick-cooking grits
1/4 cup (1/2 stick) unsalted butter
2 eggs, lightly beaten
1/2 cup (2 ounces) shredded sharp Cheddar cheese
1/4 cup (1 ounce) grated Parmesan cheese
1/4 cup (1 ounce) shredded provolone cheese
1/4 teaspoon salt
1/4 teaspoon ground red pepper

Bring the water and milk to a boil in a saucepan. Gradually add the grits and cook for 5 minutes or until thickened, stirring constantly. Remove from the heat and stir in the butter, eggs, Cheddar cheese, Parmesan cheese, provolone cheese, salt and red pepper.

Spoon the grits mixture into a 2-quart baking dish sprayed with nonstick cooking spray. Bake at 350 degrees for 40 minutes or until light brown.

Serves 6 to 8

Buttermilk Biscuits

2 cups self-rising flour
1/2 teaspoon salt
1/4 cup shortening
1/4 cup (1/2 stick) unsalted butter, softened
3/4 to 1 cup buttermilk

Mix the flour and salt in a bowl. Cut the shortening and butter into the flour mixture with a pastry blender or fork until coarse crumbs form. Blend in just enough milk with a fork until the dough leaves the side of the bowl.

Gently knead the dough on a lightly floured surface 10 to 12 times. Roll 1/2 inch thick. Cut the dough into rounds using a 2-inch cutter, dipping the cutter into additional flour between cuts. Press the cutter straight down without twisting for straight-sided, evenly shaped biscuits. Arrange the rounds 1 inch apart on a greased baking sheet. Bake at 500 degrees for 8 to 10 minutes or until light brown.

Makes 10 to 12 biscuits

Dinner Corn Bread

2 cups self-rising cornmeal mix
1/2 cup all-purpose flour
2 cups buttermilk
1 cup mild sausage, cooked and crumbled
1/4 cup chopped pimentos, drained
1/4 cup (1 ounce) shredded Cheddar cheese
1/4 cup (1/2 stick) unsalted butter, melted
1 egg, lightly beaten

Combine the cornmeal mix and flour in a bowl and mix well. Stir in the buttermilk, sausage, pimentos, cheese, butter and egg. Pour the batter into a greased cast-iron skillet and bake at 400 degrees for 20 minutes. Cut into wedges and serve.
Serves 8 to 10

Desserts

APPLE DUMPLINGS

APPLE BLUEBERRY CRISP

BERRIES AND CREAM

STRAWBERRY-BANANA CREAM CHEESE TURNOVERS

OUR FAMOUS BREAD-AND-BUTTER PUDDING

COCONUT-PINEAPPLE ICE CREAM

GEORGIA ICE CREAM

VANILLA ICE CREAM

FUDGE SAUCE

MOCHA FUDGE PUDDING

CHILLED MELON DESSERT SOUP

FRESH PEACH AND YOGURT DESSERT SOUP

TIRAMISU

OLD-FASHIONED POUND CAKE

CLASSIC CHESS PIE

COCONUT-MANGO CREAM PIE

FRESH FRUIT AND LEMON TART

KEY LIME PIE

PIE PASTRY

Favorite Desserts of the Café

Chris Crossley

I drove over to the Starfish Café where the Today Show was filming. They returned after the previous year's live broadcast (and truckloads of donations) to feature our work on a "one year later" segment. When I arrived, they were interviewing Chef Rachel, who was explaining that lives have been changed because of the program and how they were now working in restaurants throughout the community. In the background, the current class was dressed in white coats busy with preparations in the kitchen.

"Hey Mike," I heard someone whisper.

Seated at the table beside me was Chris, the graduate who was interviewed as part of the previous year's broadcast. I was struck by his transformation. He was dressed like a college prep—black T-shirt under a brownish plaid shirt, khaki pants, and loafers. Last time, his hair was naturally oily and hung limply above his eyes. Now it was brushed straight back, giving him a confident look. Beside him was an attractive woman with long black hair and large brown eyes. He introduced her as his wife and explained that she was pregnant with their first child. He still worked at Garibaldi's, though he had been promoted. They lived on Wilmington Island.

Chef Rachel completed her interview and now it was Chris's turn. As he took his place in front of the camera, his wife beamed proudly. As he spoke, I couldn't help but notice how different he looked and sounded from just a year ago. He talked with confidence and pride. He told them that the Starfish Café gave him the "second chance" that he needed so that his life could "blossom into the wonderful thing that it is now."

The video crew smiled as he said this.

I recall in the last interview, Chris explained that he had a car and how it couldn't get any better than that. Now he explained with pride how he was married and having a baby, and it couldn't get any better than that. He told them that the only television show he ever thought that he would be on was Cops. Again the crew smiled.

Chef Rachel and I watched with pride. As the interview unfolded, the lines of a song by the Eagles kept looping through my mind:

I believe in second chances
I believe in angels too
I believe in new romances
Baby I believe in you...

116

Apple Dumplings

1/4 cup (1/2 stick) unsalted butter
3/4 cup packed brown sugar
1 cup water
1 tablespoon orange juice
1/2 teaspoon ground cinnamon
1/2 teaspoon ground nutmeg
1/2 teaspoon ground cloves
1/4 teaspoon ground allspice
1 (17-ounce) package frozen puff pastry, thawed
4 Fuji apples, peeled and cored
1/3 cup granulated sugar
1/2 cup (1 stick) unsalted butter

Mix 1/4 cup butter, the brown sugar, water, orange juice, cinnamon, nutmeg, cloves and allspice in a medium saucepan. Bring to a boil and reduce the heat. Simmer for 2 minutes and remove from the heat. Roll the puff pastry sheets onto a lightly floured surface and cut into four 5-inch squares. Place one apple in the center of each square and sprinkle evenly with the granulated sugar. Dot each with 2 tablespoons butter. Pull the pastry over the apples, pinching to seal. Place in a lightly greased 9×13-inch baking dish and drizzle with the brown sugar mixture. Bake at 375 degrees for 40 to 45 minutes or until golden brown. Serve with vanilla ice cream, if desired.
Serves 4

Apple Blueberry Crisp

2 cups fresh or frozen blueberries
2 cups thinly sliced peeled Golden Delicious apples
1 tablespoon fresh lemon juice
3/4 cup packed light brown sugar
1/2 cup all-purpose flour
1/2 teaspoon ground cinnamon
3/4 cup rolled oats
1/4 cup (1/2 stick) unsalted butter or margarine,
cut into pieces and softened

Grease a shallow 1 1/2-quart baking dish with butter or margarine or spray with nonstick cooking spray. Spread the blueberries and apples evenly over the bottom of the prepared baking dish and sprinkle with the lemon juice. Mix the brown sugar, flour, cinnamon and oats in a bowl. Add the butter and mix with a fork until combined. Sprinkle evenly over the fruit. Bake at 375 degrees for 30 minutes or until bubbly and the top is golden brown. Serve warm with ice cream, if desired.

Serves 6

Berries and Cream

2 cups fresh strawberries, cut into
    quarters
1 cup fresh blueberries
1 cup fresh raspberries
1 cup fresh blackberries
1 cup peeled fresh peach chunks
1/4 cup riesling

Juice of 1 orange
4 egg yolks
Zest of 1 orange
1/3 cup sugar
1/2 cup riesling
1/2 cup heavy whipping cream
2 teaspoons vanilla extract

Combine the strawberries, blueberries, raspberries, blackberries, peaches, 1/4 cup wine and the orange juice in a medium bowl and toss to coat.

Fill a medium saucepan one-half to three-fourths full of water and bring to a strong simmer. Whisk the egg yolks, orange zest and sugar in a glass or stainless steel mixing bowl until thick and pale yellow. Stir in 1/2 cup wine. Place the bowl over but not touching the simmering water. Cook for 12 to 15 minutes or until tripled in volume, whisking constantly and adjusting the heat as needed so that the water remains at a simmer. (Do not allow the water to boil, as this will curdle the sauce.) Remove the bowl from the heat and immediately place in a medium-large bowl filled with ice water. Let stand in the ice bath for 30 minutes or until cool, stirring occasionally.

Whisk the cream and vanilla at medium-high speed in a mixing bowl until firm peaks form. Fold into the cool egg yolk mixture.

To serve, divide the berry mixture among four to six dessert bowls and spoon the orange cream over the top.

Serves 4 to 6

Strawberry-Banana Cream Cheese Turnovers

8 ounces cream cheese, softened
1/4 cup granulated sugar
Zest and juice of 1 lemon
1 teaspoon vanilla extract
1 egg, lightly beaten
2 tablespoons butter, melted
1 sheet puff pastry
1 banana, cut into slices
1 pint strawberries, finely chopped
1 1/2 cups sifted confectioners' sugar
Milk

Whisk the cream cheese, granulated sugar, lemon zest, lemon juice and vanilla in a
small mixing bowl until smooth. Mix the egg and butter in a small bowl. Place the puff
pastry on a lightly floured surface and roll with a rolling pin to smooth the surface.
Cut into six or eight squares. Brush the edges of each square with the egg mixture.
Spoon the cream cheese mixture in the center of each square and top evenly with
the banana and strawberries. Fold the opposite corners of each square together to form
a triangle. Seal the edges with a fork or your fingers. Place on a greased baking sheet
and brush the tops with the remaining egg mixture. Bake at 375 degrees for 12 minutes
or until the puff pastry has risen and is golden brown. Remove from the oven and
cool for 5 minutes.

Whisk the confectioners' sugar with enough milk to make of a thick glaze
consistency. Drizzle over the warm turnovers.

Serves 6 to 8

Our Famous Bread and Butter Pudding

Pudding

1 loaf sliced white bread, torn into
    small cubes
1 quart heavy cream
3 tablespoons unsalted butter, melted
1 tablespoon vanilla extract
1/2 cup water
1 cup golden raisins
1/2 cup raisins

3 eggs
1 1/2 cups sugar

Crème Anglaise

2/3 cup heavy cream
1/3 cup sugar
2 egg yolks
1 tablespoon vanilla extract

To prepare the pudding, mix the bread, cream, butter and vanilla in a large mixing bowl. Let stand for 10 minutes. Bring the water to a boil in a saucepan. Pour over the raisins in a medium heatproof bowl. Beat the eggs and sugar at medium-high speed in a mixing bowl for 5 minutes or until thick. Add to the bread mixture and stir to mix. Stir in the raisins. Pour into a 9×13-inch baking pan sprayed with nonstick cooking spray. Bake at 350 degrees for 45 to 60 minutes or until the pudding is golden brown and slightly set. Remove from the oven and cool on a wire rack. Chill in the refrigerator for 24 hours before serving.

To prepare the crème anglaise, bring the cream just to a boil in a saucepan over medium heat. (This usually takes 3 to 5 minutes.) Remove from the heat. Beat the sugar and egg yolks at medium-high speed in a mixing bowl for 3 minutes or until thick. Add the cream gradually, beating constantly at low speed. Return the mixture to the saucepan. Cook over medium heat for 5 to 7 minutes or until the mixture begins to thicken and coat the back of a spoon, stirring constantly. Cool in the refrigerator for 1 hour. Stir in the vanilla and return to the refrigerator until ready to serve.

    To serve, warm the bread pudding in the oven or microwave. Cut into squares and drizzle with the crème anglaise.

Serves 8 to 10

This recipe received BEST DESSERT IN SAVANNAH at the Taste of Savannah 2002.

Photograph for this recipe is shown on page 115.

Coconut Pineapple Ice Cream

1/2 gallon vanilla ice cream, softened
1 cup frozen fresh coconut flakes
1 cup canned crushed pineapple, drained
1 tablespoon spiced rum

Combine the ice cream, coconut, pineapple and rum in a large mixing bowl and mix well. Spoon into a freezer container and freeze for 2 hours or until firm.
Serves 6 to 8

This dessert is great during the summer served over grilled pound cake. Simply slice the pound cake and place it on a grill rack. Grill until grill marks appear on each side, turning once. Scoop the ice cream over the hot pound cake and enjoy.

Georgia Ice Cream

2 cups sugar
2 cups cola
4 cups half-and-half
1 teaspoon vanilla extract
1/8 teaspoon salt

Combine the sugar, cola, half-and-half, vanilla and salt in a mixing bowl and mix well. Pour into an ice cream freezer container and freeze using the manufacturer's directions.
Serves 4 to 6

Vanilla Ice Cream

3 cups heavy cream
6 egg yolks
3/4 cup sugar
1 1/2 tablespoons vanilla extract

Bring the cream to a simmer in a medium saucepan. Beat the egg yolks and sugar at medium speed in a mixing bowl until thick and pale yellow. Add the hot cream gradually, beating constantly at low speed. Return to the saucepan. Cook over low heat for 5 minutes or until the mixture is thick enough to coat the back of a spoon, whisking constantly. Remove from the heat and cool completely. Stir in the vanilla. Pour into an ice cream freezer container and freeze using the manufacturer's directions.
Serves 6 to 8

This ice cream recipe makes a good base for many variations. Try adding small pieces of brownies or sliced fresh strawberries or peaches.

Fudge Sauce

1/2 cup (3 ounces) semisweet chocolate chips
1/2 cup (1 stick) unsalted butter
1 1/2 cups heavy cream
1/2 cup confectioners' sugar, sifted
1 cup pecan pieces

Melt the chocolate chips and butter in a medium saucepan over low heat. Whisk in the cream and confectioners' sugar until completely blended. Bring to a boil and reduce the heat. Simmer for 7 minutes. Remove from the heat and stir in the pecan pieces. Serve over ice cream or pound cake.
Serves 6

Mocha Fudge Pudding

1 cup heavy cream
2 tablespoons instant espresso granules
1¹/2 cups coarsely chopped bittersweet chocolate
¹/2 cup sugar
2 eggs
2 teaspoons vanilla extract
Pinch of salt

Bring the cream and espresso granules just to a boil in a small saucepan. Remove from the heat. Combine the chocolate and sugar in a food processor and pulse until the chocolate is finely ground. Add the eggs, vanilla and salt and pulse to form a paste. Add the hot cream gradually, processing constantly for 1 minute or until the mixture is silky and smooth. Pour into individual dessert glasses and chill for 2 to 10 hours or until set. Serve with whipped cream and garnish with strawberries.
Serves 2 to 4

Chilled Melon Dessert Soup

1 cantaloupe, cut into chunks
1/2 honeydew melon, cut into chunks
4 peaches, peeled and pitted
1 tablespoon chopped mint
1 cup sour cream

1/2 cup apple juice
1/2 cup white grape juice
1/2 teaspoon salt
2 tablespoons honey

Process the cantaloupe, honeydew melon, peaches and mint in batches in a food processor until smooth. Combine the fruit mixture in a large bowl. Stir in the sour cream, apple juice, grape juice, salt and honey. Chill for 3 to 10 hours before serving.
Serves 6

Fresh Peach and Yogurt Dessert Soup

2 pounds fresh peaches
2 cups apple juice
1/4 cup honey
1 teaspoon lemon juice

1 1/2 cups plain yogurt
1/4 teaspoon ground cinnamon
1/2 cup pecan pieces, toasted

Pit and coarsely chop the unpeeled peaches. Combine the peaches, apple juice, honey and lemon juice in a stockpot. Bring to a boil and reduce the heat. Simmer for 30 minutes. Purée the peach mixture in a blender. Strain into a large bowl, discarding the solids. Chill in the refrigerator. Stir in the yogurt and cinnamon. Ladle into chilled dessert bowls and sprinkle with the pecans.
Serves 4

To toast the pecans, spread on a baking sheet and bake at 375 degrees for 3 to 4 minutes or until the pecans are light brown.

125

Tiramisu

8 ounces mascarpone cheese
1/2 cup sugar
2 1/2 cups heavy whipping cream
1 tablespoon instant coffee granules
1 cup hot water
1/4 cup coffee liqueur
2 (3-ounce) packages ladyfingers
1 teaspoon baking cocoa

Whisk the mascarpone cheese, sugar and 1/2 cup of the cream in a medium mixing bowl until smooth and creamy. Beat the remaining 2 cups cream in a mixing bowl until firm peaks form. Fold into the cheese mixture.

Dissolve the coffee granules in the hot water in a bowl. Stir in the liqueur. Dip the ladyfingers in the coffee mixture. Layer the ladyfingers and cheese mixture one-half at a time in a 9×13-inch glass dish, ending with the cheese mixture. Sprinkle with the baking cocoa. Chill for 2 hours or longer before serving.

Serves 8

You may substitute cream cheese for the mascarpone cheese.

Old-Fashioned Pound Cake

2 cups granulated sugar
1 cup (2 sticks) unsalted
    butter, softened
5 eggs
1/4 cup sour cream
1/4 cup milk

Zest of 2 lemons
1 teaspoon vanilla extract
2 1/4 cups all-purpose flour, sifted
1/2 teaspoon salt
Confectioners' sugar for sprinkling

Butter and flour a 12-cup bundt or tube pan. Beat the granulated sugar and butter at medium speed in a mixing bowl for 3 minutes or until creamy, scraping the bowl frequently. Add the eggs one at a time, beating constantly until well mixed. Beat in the sour cream, milk, lemon zest and vanilla until well mixed, scraping the bowl frequently. Add the flour and salt and beat at low speed until just moistened. Pour the batter into the prepared pan and tap the pan a few times on a flat counter to eliminate any air bubbles.

Bake at 350 degrees for 55 to 65 minutes or until a wooden pick inserted in the center comes out clean. Cool in the pan for 15 minutes. Invert onto a serving plate and cool completely. Sprinkle with confectioners' sugar, if desired.

Serves 16

To butter and flour the pan, rub softened butter evenly over the entire inside surface of the pan. Scoop a few spoonfuls of all-purpose flour in the pan and shake the pan until the flour coats all the buttered surfaces. Turn the pan upside down and tap the pan to remove any excess flour.

Classic Chess Pie

4 cups sugar
1/4 cup cornmeal
2 tablespoons all-purpose flour
1/2 teaspoon salt
1 cup (2 sticks) unsalted butter, melted
8 eggs, lightly beaten
1/2 cup milk
2 tablespoons white vinegar
1 teaspoon vanilla extract
2 baked (9-inch) pie shells

Mix the sugar, cornmeal, flour and salt in a large mixing bowl. Combine the butter, eggs, milk, vinegar and vanilla in a medium mixing bowl and mix well. Add to the dry ingredients and whisk until well combined. Divide the batter between the baked pie shells. Wrap the edges with foil to prevent overbrowning. Bake at 350 degrees for 50 to 55 minutes or until set, removing the foil during the last 5 to 10 minutes. Cool completely on a wire rack.
Makes 2 pies

Try baking your own piecrusts from our Pie Pastry recipe on page 131.

Coconut-Mango Cream Pie

1 unbaked (10-inch) deep-dish pie
   shell
1/2 cup sugar
1/4 cup cornstarch
2 cups half-and-half
4 egg yolks
3 tablespoons butter

1 cup sweetened flaked coconut
1 teaspoon vanilla extract
1 large mango, peeled and thinly sliced
2 cups heavy whipping cream
1/2 cup shredded coconut, toasted
1 1/2 teaspoons vanilla extract

Bake the pie shell at 350 degrees for 5 minutes or until golden brown. Remove from the oven to cool.

Mix the sugar and cornstarch in a heavy saucepan. Whisk the half-and-half and egg yolks in a mixing bowl. Add to the sugar mixture gradually, whisking constantly. Bring to a boil over medium heat, whisking constantly. Boil for 1 minute. Remove from the heat. Stir in the butter, flaked coconut and 1 teaspoon vanilla. Cover with plastic wrap, placing the plastic wrap directly on the filling. Let stand for 30 minutes.

Layer the mango slices in the cooled pie shell. Spoon the filling over the mango slices. Chill for 30 minutes or until set.

Beat the whipping cream at high speed in a mixing bowl until medium peaks begin to form. Stir in the toasted coconut and 1 1/2 teaspoons vanilla. Spread or pipe over the pie.

Serves 8

Fresh Fruit and Lemon Tart

Tart Crust
1¹/4 cups all-purpose flour
1 tablespoon confectioners' sugar
¹/4 teaspoon salt
¹/2 cup (1 stick) unsalted butter,
    chilled and cut into pieces
1 egg yolk, beaten
2 to 3 tablespoons cold water

Tart
3 egg yolks
²/3 cup sugar

4 teaspoons cornstarch
¹/4 cup lemon juice
1 teaspoon lemon zest
¹/4 cup water
¹/4 cup (¹/2 stick) unsalted butter
1 tablespoon apricot jelly
3 cups assorted fresh fruit, such as
    sliced strawberries, blueberries,
    raspberries, sliced pineapple,
    sliced peaches and sliced
    kiwifruit

To prepare the crust, mix the flour, confectioners' sugar and salt in a medium bowl. Add the butter and mix with your fingers until the mixture resembles coarse crumbs. Stir in the egg yolk and enough cold water to hold the dough together. Shape the dough into a ball. Roll the dough into an 11-inch circle on a lightly floured surface. Fit into a greased 9-inch tart pan with a removable bottom, trimming the excess pastry. Prick the bottom and side with a fork. Bake at 425 degrees for 15 to 18 minutes or until light brown. Remove from the oven to cool completely.

To prepare the tart, beat the egg yolks in a medium mixing bowl. Mix the sugar and cornstarch in a 1-quart saucepan. Stir in the lemon juice, lemon zest and water. Cook over medium-high heat for 2 to 3 minutes or until the mixture comes to a boil, stirring constantly. Remove from the heat. Stir one-half of the hot mixture into the egg yolks. Return the mixture to the saucepan. Cook over low heat for 2 to 3 minutes or until the mixture boils and thickens, stirring constantly. Remove from the heat. Stir in the butter. Cover the surface with plastic wrap. Chill for 1 hour or longer. Microwave the jelly in a microwave-safe bowl on High for 20 to 30 seconds or until melted. Spread the filling in the tart crust. Arrange the fruit over the filling. Brush the fruit with the melted jelly.
Serves 8 to 10

Key Lime Pie

1 (14-ounce) can sweetened condensed milk
3 egg yolks
1/2 cup fresh lime juice
2 teaspoons grated lime zest (zest from about 2 limes)
1 (9-inch) graham cracker pie shell

Process the condensed milk, egg yolks, lime juice and lime zest in a blender until smooth. Pour into the pie shell. Bake at 350 degrees for 8 to 10 minutes or until set to a gelatin consistency. Remove from the oven to cool completely. Cut into wedges and garnish with lime wedges.

Serves 6

Pie Pastry

2 1/2 cups all-purpose flour
1 tablespoon sugar
1 teaspoon salt
1/2 cup (1 stick) unsalted butter, chilled and cut into small cubes
1/2 cup vegetable shortening, chilled
2 tablespoons lemon juice
2 to 3 tablespoons cold water

Mix the flour, sugar and salt in a large bowl. Cut in the butter and shortening with a pastry cutter or your fingers until the mixture resembles coarse cornmeal. Stir in the lemon juice and just enough of the cold water to form a ball. Divide the dough into halves. Shape each half into a disk and wrap in plastic wrap. Chill for 1 hour before using or store in the freezer for up to 1 month.

Makes two 9-inch pie crusts

Holidays

Holiday Quiche

Potato, Bacon and Pea Frittata

Garden Omelet

Savannah Omelet

Seafood Omelet

Fresh Fruit Bruschetta

Ginger-Glazed Fruit

Fruited Poached Pears

Hot Chocolate

Spiced Apple Cider

Hot Spiced Cider with
Cinnamon-Honey Butter

Sparkling Lemonade

French Mimosas

Baked Brie

Chicken Almond Cream Soup

Creamy Butternut Squash and
Ginger-Apple Soup

Apple and Cranberry-Stuffed Pork
Chops with Roasted Root Vegetables

Pan-Roasted Turkey with Cranberry
Orange Relish

Baklava

New York-Style Cheesecake

Marbled Pumpkin Cheesecake

Double-Decker Raspberry and White
Chocolate Cheesecake

Chocolate Crème Brûlée

Lemon Crème Brûlée with Fresh Berries

Black and White Chocolate Mousse
with Fresh Raspberries

Fresh Raspberry Shortcakes

Carrot Cake with Cream
Cheese Frosting

Gingerbread Cake

Chocolate Fudge

Cranberry-Orange Chocolate Truffles

Gingersnaps

Almond Spice Cookies

Harvest Cookies

Pumpkin Pie

Celebrating Holidays at the Café

Lelia Wilson

Jeffersonville, Georgia, is a small rural town, but that doesn't mean that kids can't get into trouble. By the time that Lelia was fifteen, she was causing confusion in her home and using drugs. Somehow, she did manage to graduate from high school, but dropped out of vocational college when her addiction demanded too much of her time. She drifted from job to job, always losing them because she failed to show up or when she did she wasn't herself. A daughter was born by the time Lelia was twenty-five, but she left the girl with her parents and moved in with her grandmother. She continued her addiction and spent several nights in jail. She got pregnant again, and her parents took her son when he was born. Lelia ended up doing significant time in jail after her parents called the police and reported her for theft. There wasn't much further down that Lelia could fall.

Upon release, she entered treatment and moved into Union Mission's program for women in recovery, where she stayed for two years. She worked ten different jobs the first year that she lived there.

Then Phyllis Nichols, her case manager, suggested that she and another resident team up and enroll in the Starfish Café. Lelia took to the culinary arts education and the restaurant experience. It seemed that no time had passed, yet here she was graduating.

"I finally finished something in my life," she explains with tears in her eyes. "I finally accomplished something."

Since graduation, Lelia has consistently worked preparing food for the homeless in shelters. "It reminds me of where I've come from," she explains, "and that I could go back again if I am not careful."

She returns to tiny Jeffersonville to visit her children and her parents each month. She calls her kids everyday. The children visit her each summer.

As she tells me this, she prepares to have her photograph taken for the cookbook. She looks at me with a tearful, yet happy, smile.

"You know, being homeless…being an addict…I'm sitting here today with three chefs, getting my picture taken for a cookbook. Who would have ever thought? Everyone always told me that I would amount to nothing; I am proud of myself!"

Holiday Quiche

Crust
1 cup all-purpose flour
1/4 teaspoon salt
1/3 cup unsalted butter
2 tablespoons chopped fresh chives
2 tablespoons cold water

Filling
2 cups cubed Brie cheese
1 cup cooked crumbled
     breakfast sausage

6 slices bacon, crisp-cooked and
     broken into 1-inch pieces
4 ounces fresh asparagus spears
1 1/2 cups milk
8 eggs, lightly beaten
1/4 teaspoon salt
1/8 teaspoon pepper

To prepare the crust, mix the flour and salt in a bowl. Cut in the butter using a pastry blender or fork until coarse crumbs form. Add the chives and water and stir just until moistened; the mixture will be crumbly. Shape the dough into a ball and flatten slightly.

Roll the dough into 1/8-inch-thick 12-inch circle on a lightly floured surface. Fold into quarters and place in a 10-inch quiche pan. Unfold the dough and press firmly over the bottom and side of the pan. Trim the crust to 1/2 inch from the edge of the pan. Crimp or flute the edge.

To prepare the filling, sprinkle the cheese, sausage and bacon in the order listed over the bottom of the crust. Arrange the asparagus spears in a spoke pattern over the prepared layers. Whisk the milk, eggs, salt and pepper in a bowl until blended and pour over the top. Bake at 400 degrees for 45 to 60 minutes or until the center is set and the top is golden brown. Let stand for 10 minutes before serving.
Serves 6 to 8

For a quick version, use a commercially-prepared pie shell.

Potato, Bacon and Pea Frittata

2 teaspoons olive oil
8 ounces potatoes, shredded
4 slices bacon, finely chopped
1/4 cup frozen peas, thawed
1 garlic clove, minced
4 egg whites
2 eggs
Salt and pepper to taste
1/4 cup (1 ounce) shredded Parmesan cheese

Heat the olive oil in a medium to large heatproof skillet and add the potatoes and bacon. Sauté until golden brown. Stir in the peas and garlic and cook for 1 minute. Remove from the heat.

Whisk the egg whites, eggs, salt and pepper in a bowl until blended. Pour the egg mixture over the potato mixture, tilting the pan to ensure even coverage. Bake at 350 degrees just until the eggs are set. Sprinkle with the cheese and bake just until the cheese melts. Cut into wedges and serve immediately.

Serves 4 to 6

Garden Omelet

1 tablespoon olive oil
1/4 cup finely chopped red bell pepper
1/4 cup finely chopped zucchini
1/4 cup finely chopped yellow squash
2 tablespoons finely chopped
   purple onion
Salt and pepper to taste
4 eggs, lightly beaten
2 tablespoons milk

1 tablespoon chopped fresh
   Italian parsley
1/4 cup (1 ounce) shredded buffalo
   mozzarella cheese
1 tablespoon grated Parmesan cheese
1/2 vine-ripe tomato, seeded and
   finely chopped
1 tablespoon chopped fresh chives

Heat the olive oil in a sauté pan over medium-high heat and add the bell pepper, zucchini, yellow squash and onion. Sauté for 3 minutes and season with salt and pepper.

Whisk the eggs, milk and parsley in a bowl until combined. Season with salt and pepper. Heat an 8-inch nonstick sauté pan over medium heat and coat with nonstick cooking spray. Add half the egg mixture to the hot pan, tilting the pan to ensure even coverage.

As the egg mixture begins to cook, gently lift the edge of the omelet with a spatula to allow the uncooked egg to flow underneath. Continue cooking and lifting the edge of the omelet until almost all of the egg is cooked.

Sprinkle half the omelet with half the mozzarella cheese, half the sautéed vegetable mixture and half the Parmesan cheese. Season with salt and pepper and fold the plain side over the filling. Remove the omelet to a heated plate and repeat the process with the remaining egg mixture, remaining mozzarella cheese, remaining sautéed vegetables and remaining Parmesan cheese. Sprinkle each omelet evenly with the tomato and chives and serve.

Serves 2

Savannah Omelet

1/2 vine-ripe tomato, seeded and finely chopped
1/4 cup chopped pecans, toasted
1 teaspoon honey
1 tablespoon canola oil
3/4 cup chopped country ham
1/4 cup finely chopped Vidalia onion
Salt and pepper to taste
4 eggs, lightly beaten
2 tablespoons milk
1/2 cup (2 ounces) shredded sharp Cheddar cheese

Mix the tomato, pecans and honey in a bowl. Heat the canola oil in a sauté pan over medium-high heat. Sauté the ham and onion in the hot oil for 2 minutes. Season with salt and pepper. Whisk the eggs and milk in a bowl until blended.

Heat an 8-inch nonstick sauté pan over medium heat and coat with nonstick cooking spray. Add half the egg mixture to the hot pan, tilting the pan to ensure even coverage. As the egg mixture begins to cook, gently lift the edge of the omelet with a spatula to allow the uncooked egg to flow underneath. Continue cooking and lifting the edge of the omelet until almost all of the egg is cooked. Sprinkle half the omelet with half the cheese and half the ham mixture. Season with salt and pepper and fold the plain side over the filling. Remove the omelet to a heated plate and repeat the process with the remaining egg mixture, remaining cheese and remaining ham mixture. Top each omelet with half the tomato mixture before serving.

Serves 2

Seafood Omelet

4 eggs, lightly beaten
2 tablespoons milk
Salt and pepper to taste
1/4 cup (1 ounce) shredded smoked Gouda cheese
1/4 cup crab meat
2 sea scallops, cooked and finely chopped
1/4 cup cooked shrimp, finely chopped
1 tablespoon grated Parmesan cheese
1/2 vine-ripe tomato, seeded and finely chopped
1 tablespoon chopped fresh chives

Whisk the eggs and milk in a small bowl until blended. Season with salt and pepper. Heat an 8-inch nonstick sauté pan over medium heat and coat with nonstick cooking spray. Add half the egg mixture to the hot pan, tilting the pan to ensure even coverage. As the egg mixture begins to cook, gently lift the edge of the omelet with a spatula to allow the uncooked egg to flow underneath. Continue cooking and lifting the edge of the omelet until almost all of the egg is cooked.

Sprinkle half the omelet with half the Gouda cheese, half the crab meat, half the scallops, half the shrimp and half the Parmesan cheese. Season with salt and pepper and fold the plain side over the filling. Remove the omelet to a heated plate and repeat the process with the remaining egg mixture, remaining Gouda cheese, remaining crab meat, remaining scallops, remaining shrimp and remaining Parmesan cheese. Top each omelet with equal portions of the tomato and chives and serve.
Serves 2

Fresh Fruit Bruschetta

1/2 cup finely chopped mango
1/2 cup finely chopped pineapple
1/2 cup finely chopped peach
1/2 cup finely chopped strawberries
1/4 cup finely chopped kiwifruit
1/4 cup finely chopped cherries
1/4 cup sugar
1 tablespoon chopped fresh mint
1 French baguette, cut into 1/4-inch slices
Melted butter
Cinnamon-sugar to taste

Combine the mango, pineapple, peach, strawberries, kiwifruit, cherries, sugar and mint in a medium bowl and mix gently. Brush the baguette slices with butter and sprinkle with cinnamon-sugar.

Arrange the slices in a single layer on a baking sheet and bake at 375 degrees until golden brown and crisp. Top each bread slice with a heaping portion of the fresh fruit mixture.

Serves 6 to 8

Substitute as desired with any combination of fresh fruit.

Ginger-Glazed Fruit

3 tablespoons sugar
2 teaspoons cornstarch
Dash of salt
1/2 cup apple juice
1/2 teaspoon lemon juice
1/4 teaspoon grated fresh ginger
6 cups chopped fresh fruit (such as cantaloupe, strawberries,
    pineapple, bananas, and apples)
1 tablespoon chopped fresh mint

Combine the sugar, cornstarch and salt in a 1-quart saucepan and mix well. Stir in the apple juice, lemon juice and ginger. Cook over medium heat for 7 to 8 minutes or until the mixture comes to a boil, stirring constantly. Boil for 1 minute. Remove from the heat and let stand until cool. Combine the fruit and dressing in a bowl and mix gently until coated. Stir in the mint.
Serves 6

Fruited Poached Pears

5 cups apple cider
1/2 cup golden raisins
1/2 cup dried cranberries
1/2 cup sugar
1/4 cup raspberry preserves
3 cinnamon sticks
1 tablespoon whole cloves
1 tablespoon whole allspice
1 teaspoon vanilla extract
4 firm ripe pears, cut into quarters
Vanilla ice cream

Combine the cider, raisins, cranberries, sugar, preserves, cinnamon sticks, cloves, allspice and vanilla in a large saucepan and bring to a boil. Reduce the heat to low and bring the poaching liquid to a simmer. Add the pears to the hot liquid and simmer for 10 to 12 minutes or until tender. Discard the cinnamon sticks, cloves and allspice.

Divide the pears evenly among four dessert bowls. Spoon the cranberries and raisins over the pears and drizzle evenly with the remaining poaching liquid. Top each serving with a scoop of ice cream and serve immediately.
Serves 4

Hot Chocolate

5 cups milk
1¹/2 cups (9 ounces) semisweet chocolate chips
1 teaspoon vanilla extract
Pinch of nutmeg

Combine the milk and chocolate chips in a medium saucepan. Cook over low to medium heat until the chocolate melts. Remove from the heat and stir in the vanilla and nutmeg. Pour the hot chocolate into mugs and serve plain or topped with marshmallows and/or whipped cream.
Serves 4

Spiced Apple Cider

6 cups apple cider
1 orange, thinly sliced
2 tablespoons whole cloves
3 cinnamon sticks

Combine the cider, orange slices, cloves and cinnamon sticks in a stockpot and simmer for 30 minutes. Discard the orange slices, cloves and cinnamon sticks. Ladle the warm cider into mugs and garnish with additional orange slices.
Serves 6

Hot Spiced Cider with Cinnamon-Honey Butter

Cinnamon-Honey Butter
6 tablespoons unsalted butter, softened
1 tablespoon honey
1/4 teaspoon vanilla extract
1/4 teaspoon ground cinnamon

Spiced Cider
6 cups apple cider or apple juice
20 whole cloves
3 cinnamon sticks
8 slices crystallized ginger

To prepare the butter, mix the butter, honey, vanilla and cinnamon in a bowl until blended.

To prepare the spiced cider, combine the cider, cloves, cinnamon sticks and ginger in a heavy saucepan. Bring to a boil over medium-high heat and reduce the heat to low.

Simmer, covered, for 30 minutes. Strain, discarding the solids. Ladle the hot cider into mugs or cups. Stir 1 tablespoon of the cinnamon-honey butter into each serving and serve immediately.

Serves 6

Sparkling Lemonade

Juice of 9 large lemons
3/4 cup confectioners' sugar
6 cups sparkling water, chilled

Combine the lemon juice and confectioners' sugar in a pitcher and stir until the confectioners' sugar dissolves. Chill until serving time. Stir in the sparkling water. Pour the lemonade over ice in glasses and garnish each serving with lemon slices.
Serves 6

French Mimosas

Chambord to taste
Sugar to taste
1 quart (4 cups) orange juice
1/2 cup Chambord
1 (750-milliliter) bottle Champagne, chilled
Fresh raspberries

Pour liqueur to taste and sugar into separate flat shallow dishes. Moisten the rims of 6 to 8 glasses with the liqueur. Dip each moistened rim in the sugar and rotate gently to cover the rims evenly. This process may be accomplished well in advance of serving.

Combine the orange juice and 1/2 cup liqueur in a large pitcher and mix well. Stir in the Champagne. Place a few raspberries in each prepared glass and pour the mimosa mixture over the raspberries. Serve immediately.
Serves 6 to 8

Baked Brie

1/2 cup packed brown sugar
1/4 cup finely chopped dried apples
1/4 cup dried cranberries
1/4 cup golden raisins
1/4 cup dried blueberries
2 tablespoons orange juice
1 (8-ounce) round Brie cheese

Mix the brown sugar, apples, cranberries, raisins, blueberries and orange juice in a medium saucepan and bring to a boil, stirring occasionally. Remove from the heat and let stand until room temperature.

Arrange the Brie on a baking sheet and heat at 325 degrees for 5 minutes. Spoon the fruit mixture over the warm Brie and serve with assorted party crackers and/or toast rounds.
Serves 4

Chicken Almond Cream Soup

2 tablespoons unsalted butter
1/2 yellow onion, finely chopped
1/4 cup button mushrooms, sliced
1 rib celery, finely chopped
2 tablespoons all-purpose flour
1 quart (4 cups) chicken broth
1 cup heavy cream
2 boneless skinless chicken breasts, grilled and finely chopped
1/4 cup almonds, toasted and crushed
1 tablespoon Worcestershire sauce
Salt and pepper to taste

Melt the butter in a stockpot over medium heat and add the onion, mushrooms and celery. Cook for 2 minutes, stirring frequently. Add the flour and cook for 1 minute, stirring constantly. Whisk in the broth and cream gradually.

Bring the soup to a simmer and stir in the chicken and almonds. Cook over medium-low heat for 20 minutes, stirring occasionally. Stir in the Worcestershire sauce and season with salt and pepper. Ladle into soup bowls.

Serves 4

Creamy Butternut Squash and Ginger Apple Soup

1 tablespoon unsalted butter
1/2 cup chopped yellow onion
1 (2-pound) butternut squash, chopped into 1-inch pieces
4 cups low-sodium chicken broth
2 teaspoons minced fresh ginger
2 Granny Smith apples, peeled and chopped
2 pinches of Spanish saffron threads
Pinch of freshly grated nutmeg
Pinch of ground cinnamon
1 cup plain yogurt
Salt and freshly ground pepper to taste

Melt the butter in a stockpot over medium heat and add the onion. Sauté for 4 to 6 minutes or until the onion is tender, stirring occasionally. Add the squash, broth and ginger and bring to a boil. Reduce the heat to medium-low.

Simmer for 20 minutes or until the squash is fork-tender. Stir in the apples, saffron, nutmeg and cinnamon. Simmer for 15 minutes or until the apples are tender, stirring occasionally.

Process the soup in batches in a food processor or blender until puréed. Return the purée to the stockpot and stir in the yogurt. Season with salt and pepper. Reheat over low heat and ladle into soup bowls.

Serves 6

Apple and Cranberry-Stuffed Pork Chops with Roasted Root Vegetables

Pork Chops and Stuffing

3 tablespoons butter
1/2 cup finely chopped yellow onion
1/2 cup finely chopped celery
1/4 cup pine nuts
1 1/2 cups herb-seasoned stuffing mix
1 (14-ounce) can chicken broth
1/2 cup finely chopped Granny
    Smith apple
1/4 cup golden raisins
1/4 cup dried cranberries
6 tablespoons minced Italian parsley
1/4 cup packed brown sugar
5 fresh sage leaves, finely chopped
1/2 teaspoon each salt and black pepper
1/4 teaspoon ground red pepper

6 (2-inch-thick) bone-in center-cut
    pork chops
1/2 teaspoon each salt and black pepper
1/4 cup olive oil
1 cup water

Roasted Root Vegetables

1 pound parsnips, coarsely chopped
3 large beets, coarsely chopped
2 large turnips, coarsely chopped
2 large sweet potatoes, coarsely chopped
1 large rutabaga, coarsely chopped
1 yellow onion, coarsely chopped
1 carrot, coarsely chopped
1 teaspoon each salt and pepper
2 tablespoons unsalted butter, melted

To prepare the pork chops, melt the butter in a large skillet over medium-high heat and add the onion, celery and pine nuts. Sauté for 5 to 7 minutes or until the onion and celery are tender and the pine nuts are golden brown. Remove from the heat and add the stuffing mix and broth, stirring until the broth is absorbed. Stir in the apple, raisins, cranberries, parsley, brown sugar, sage, 1/2 teaspoon salt, 1/2 teaspoon black pepper and the red pepper. Let stand for 30 minutes.

Trim any excess fat from the pork chops and make a slit in the side of each chop to form a pocket. Spoon the stuffing mixture evenly into the pockets. Rub the surface of the pork chops with a mixture of 1/2 teaspoon salt and 1/2 teaspoon black pepper. Heat 2 tablespoons of the olive oil in a large nonstick skillet over medium-high heat. Sear three of the stuffed pork chops in the hot oil for 2 minutes per side or until brown. Arrange the pork chops on a lightly greased rack in a broiler pan. Repeat the process with the remaining 2 tablespoons olive oil and three stuffed pork chops. Pour the water into the broiler pan and bake at 375 degrees for 30 to 40 minutes or until the pork chops are cooked through. Let stand for 5 minutes before serving.

To prepare the vegetables, coat two foil-lined baking sheets with nonstick cooking spray. Arrange the vegetables in a single layer on the prepared baking sheets. Lightly coat the vegetables with nonstick cooking spray and sprinkle with the salt and pepper. Bake at 425 degrees for 35 to 45 minutes or until the vegetables are tender, turning the pans after 15 to 20 minutes to ensure even roasting. Drizzle with the butter and toss to coat. Serve with the pork chops.

Serves 6

Pan-Roasted Turkey with Cranberry Orange Relish

Roasted Turkey

1 tablespoon parsley flakes
1 teaspoon dried thyme
1/2 teaspoon dried rosemary
1/2 teaspoon dried sage
6 boneless skinless turkey breast
   tenderloins
Salt and pepper to taste
1/4 cup olive oil
2 tablespoons unsalted butter
1 cup chicken broth

Cranberry Orange Relish

1/2 cup water
1 cup fresh cranberries
1/2 cup sugar
1/4 cup orange juice
Grated zest of 1 orange

To prepare the turkey, mix the parsley flakes, thyme, rosemary and sage in a small bowl. Season each tenderloin with salt and pepper and rub with the herb mixture. Heat the olive oil and butter in a large skillet over medium-high heat and add the tenderloins. Sauté until brown on each side. Arrange the tenderloins in a single layer in a 9×13-inch baking dish. Pour the broth over the top and roast at 350 degrees until the tenderloins are cooked through; the cooking time will vary depending on the thickness. Let stand for 3 minutes and then cut into strips.

To prepare the relish, bring the water to a simmer in a medium saucepan. Add the cranberries, sugar, orange juice and orange zest and mix well. Cook for 15 minutes or until the sugar dissolves and the cranberries begin to pop, stirring constantly. Remove from the heat and spoon the warm relish over the tenderloin strips.

Serves 6

Baklava

3 cups finely chopped walnuts
2 tablespoons brown sugar
2 teaspoons ground cinnamon
$1/2$ teaspoon ground cloves
$1/4$ teaspoon ground allspice
1 (16-ounce) package phyllo pastry, thawed
$1^1/4$ cups ($2^1/2$ sticks) unsalted butter, melted
2 cups sugar
1 cup water
2 tablespoons orange juice

Combine the walnuts, brown sugar, cinnamon, cloves and allspice in a bowl and mix well. Unroll the phyllo and immediately cover with plastic wrap and a damp towel to prevent drying out, removing one sheet at a time.

Brush a 9×13-inch baking pan with some of the butter. Lay 1 sheet of the pastry in the prepared baking pan and lightly brush with butter. Layer with another sheet of the pastry and brush with butter. Repeat the process six more times for a total of 8 sheets, brushing each layer with butter. Sprinkle with half the walnut mixture.

Layer another 8 sheets of the pastry over the walnut mixture, brushing each layer with butter. Sprinkle with the remaining walnut mixture. Top with 8 more sheets of pastry, brushing each layer with butter. Using a sharp knife, score diagonally $1/4$-inch-deep through the layers into 2-inch diamonds. Bake at 350 degrees for 40 minutes or until golden brown. Cool in the pan on a wire rack for 5 to 10 minutes.

Combine the sugar, water and orange juice in a saucepan and bring to a boil over high heat. Reduce the heat to low and simmer for 3 to 4 minutes, stirring occasionally. Pour the hot syrup over the prepared layers and let stand until cool. Using a sharp knife, slice all the way through the scoring into diamond-shaped bars.

Makes 4 dozen bars

New York-Style Cheesecake

Butter for coating
20 ounces cream cheese, softened
3/4 cup sugar
1 tablespoon all-purpose flour
4 eggs, lightly beaten
1/4 cup heavy cream
1 tablespoon vanilla extract

Line the bottom of a 10-inch springform pan with waxed paper and coat the waxed paper and side of the pan with butter. Beat the cream cheese in the mixing bowl of an electric mixer fitted with a whisk attachment at medium speed until light and fluffy, scraping the bowl occasionally. Add the sugar and flour and beat until combined.

Reduce the speed to low and add the eggs, cream and vanilla in the order listed, beating until combined after each addition. Pour the batter into the prepared pan and bake at 300 degrees for 1 to 1¹/2 hours or until set. Cool in the pan on a wire rack. Store, covered, in the refrigerator.

Makes 1 (10-inch) cheesecake

Marbled Pumpkin Cheesecake

Graham Cracker Crust
Butter for coating
1 1/4 cups graham cracker crumbs
1/4 cup (1/2 stick) unsalted butter,
    melted
2 tablespoons sugar
6 tablespoons miniature chocolate
    chips

Cheesecake
6 tablespoons semisweet chocolate chips
24 ounces cream cheese, softened
1 cup granulated sugar
1/4 cup packed brown sugar
1 (15-ounce) can pumpkin purée
4 eggs
1/2 cup evaporated milk
2 tablespoons cornstarch
1 teaspoon ground cinnamon
1/8 teaspoon ground nutmeg

To prepare the crust, line the bottom of a 9-inch springform pan with waxed paper and coat the waxed paper and side of the pan with butter. Wrap the outside of the pan with foil. Mix the graham cracker crumbs, 1/4 cup butter and the sugar in a bowl. Pat the crumb mixture over the bottom of the prepared pan and sprinkle with the chocolate chips.

To prepare the cheesecake, place the chocolate chips in a microwave-safe dish and microwave until smooth. Beat the cream cheese, granulated sugar and brown sugar in a mixing bowl at medium-high speed for 3 minutes or until creamy. Reduce the speed to medium and add the pumpkin. Beat until combined. Add the eggs one at a time, beating well after each addition. Add the evaporated milk, cornstarch, cinnamon and nutmeg and mix well.

Reserve 1 cup of the batter. Pour the remaining batter into the prepared pan. Combine the reserved 1 cup batter and the melted chocolate in a bowl and mix well. Swirl into the top of the prepared layer. Place the cheesecake in a large baking pan and pour enough warm water around the springform pan to measure 1 inch. Bake at 325 degrees for 1 1/2 hours or until the edge is set and the center moves slightly. Cool in the pan on a wire rack for 1 hour. Chill, covered, for 8 to 10 hours before serving.
Makes 1 (9-inch) cheesecake

Double-Decker Raspberry and White Chocolate Cheesecake

Chocolate Cookie Crust
1 (9-ounce) package chocolate wafer
    cookies, coarsely broken
2 tablespoons unsalted butter, melted

Cheesecake
1 (12-ounce) package frozen
    unsweetened raspberries, thawed
3/4 cup finely chopped white chocolate

32 ounces cream cheese, softened
1 1/3 cups sugar
2 tablespoons all-purpose flour
4 eggs
2 tablespoons heavy cream
2 teaspoons vanilla extract
1/2 teaspoon almond extract

To prepare the crust, process the cookies in a food processor until coarse crumbs form. Add the butter and process until evenly moistened. Press the crumb mixture over the bottom of a greased 9-inch springform pan. Bake at 325 degrees for 8 minutes. Cool on a wire rack. Maintain the oven temperature.

To prepare the cheesecake, press the raspberries through a fine mesh strainer into a small bowl, discarding the pulp and seeds. Reserve 1/2 cup of the purée, using the remaining purée for another purpose. Place the white chocolate in a microwave-safe dish and microwave just until melted.

Beat the cream cheese and sugar in a mixing bowl at medium speed for 4 minutes or until smooth and fluffy, scraping the bowl occasionally. Add the flour and beat at low speed until blended. Add the eggs one at a time, beating well after each addition. Blend in the cream and flavorings.

Mix 2 1/4 cups of the batter with the white chocolate in a bowl. Stir the reserved 1/2 cup raspberry purée into the remaining batter. Pour the raspberry batter over the crust. Arrange the pan in a large baking dish and pour enough hot water into the baking dish to measure 1/2 inch. Bake for 50 minutes or just until the center is set and the edge is beginning to puff. Remove from the oven and cool for 5 minutes or until slightly firm. Gently spoon the white chocolate batter over the baked layer and bake for 30 minutes longer. Remove the pan to a wire rack to cool. Chill, covered, for 4 hours or longer before serving.

Makes 1 (9-inch) cheesecake

To unmold the cheesecake from the springform pan, run a thin sharp knife along the edge of the cheesecake and then remove the side.

Chocolate Crème Brûlée

6 ounces semisweet chocolate
2 cups whipping cream
5 egg yolks
1/2 cup sugar
1 teaspoon vanilla extract
1/2 cup sugar

Combine the chocolate and cream in a small heavy saucepan. Cook over low heat until the chocolate melts, stirring occasionally. Beat the egg yolks and 1/2 cup sugar in a mixing bowl until thick and pale yellow. Pour the chocolate mixture into the egg yolk mixture and beat at low speed until blended.

   Return the chocolate mixture to the saucepan and cook over medium-low heat for 5 to 7 minutes or until the mixture coats the back of a spoon, whisking constantly. Remove from the heat and stir in the vanilla.

   Divide the custard evenly among six crème brûlée dishes. Arrange the dishes in a large baking pan and add enough water to the baking pan to reach halfway up the sides of the dishes. Bake at 300 degrees for 45 minutes or until set. Let stand in the water bath until cool enough to handle. Chill for 24 hours. Sprinkle 1/2 cup sugar evenly over the tops and arrange the dishes on a baking sheet. Broil until brown.
Serves 6

Lemon Crème Brûlée with Fresh Berries

3 cups heavy cream
1 vanilla bean, split into halves
Grated zest of 4 lemons
3/4 cup granulated sugar
6 egg yolks
1/4 teaspoon salt
Light brown sugar for sprinkling

1 pint fresh raspberries
1 pint fresh strawberries,
    cut into quarters
1 pint fresh blackberries,
    cut into halves
1/4 cup Chambord

Arrange eight 3/4-cup custard cups or ramekins in a 9×13-inch baking pan. Mix the cream, vanilla bean and lemon zest in a small heavy saucepan and bring to a simmer. Beat the granulated sugar and egg yolks in a mixing bowl at medium speed for 3 minutes or until thick and pale yellow. Remove the vanilla bean from the cream mixture and reserve. Gradually pour the hot cream mixture into the egg mixture, beating constantly until blended. Scrape the seeds out of the vanilla bean using the back of a knife and mix the seeds into the egg mixture, discarding the pod. Stir in the salt.

Divide the custard evenly among the custard cups. Pour enough hot water into the baking pan to reach halfway up the sides of the cups. Bake at 325 degrees for 55 minutes or just until set. Remove the custards from the water bath and chill, uncovered, until firm. You may store in the refrigerator for up to 2 days.

Arrange the custard cups on a baking sheet and sprinkle with brown sugar. Broil for 2 minutes or until the brown sugar melts and browns. Toss the raspberries, strawberries and blackberries with the liqueur in a bowl. Serve the berry mixture in a bowl on the side or spoon over the tops of the custards.

Serves 8

Black and White Chocolate Mousse with Fresh Raspberries

Black Chocolate Mousse
1/4 cup whipping cream
8 ounces semisweet baking chocolate, coarsely broken
1/4 cup light corn syrup
1/4 cup (1/2 stick) butter
3/4 cup whipping cream
2 tablespoons confectioners' sugar
1/2 teaspoon vanilla extract

White Chocolate Mousse and Assembly
2 tablespoons whipping cream
3 ounces white baking chocolate, coarsely broken
2 tablespoons light corn syrup
2 tablespoons butter
6 tablespoons whipping cream
1 tablespoon confectioners' sugar
1/4 teaspoon vanilla extract
2 cups fresh raspberries

To prepare the black chocolate mousse, combine 1/4 cup cream, the chocolate, corn syrup and butter in a microwave-safe bowl. Microwave until the chocolate melts and then stir. Let stand until cool. Beat 3/4 cup cream, the confectioners' sugar and vanilla in a mixing bowl at high speed until stiff peaks form and then fold into the chocolate mixture. Chill, covered, for 1 hour or longer.

To prepare the white chocolate mousse, combine 2 tablespoons cream, the white chocolate, corn syrup and butter in a microwave-safe bowl. Microwave until the chocolate melts and then stir. Let stand until cool. Beat 6 tablespoons cream, the confectioners' sugar and vanilla in a mixing bowl at high speed until stiff peaks form and then fold into the white chocolate mixture. Chill, covered, for 1 hour or longer.

Divide half the black chocolate mousse evenly among four dessert cups. Layer with half the raspberries, the white chocolate mousse, the remaining raspberries and the remaining black chocolate mousse. Serve immediately.

Serves 4

Fresh Raspberry Shortcakes

Raspberry Topping
4 cups raspberries
1/4 cup sugar
Grated zest of 1 orange

Whipped Cream
3/4 cup heavy whipping cream, chilled
2 tablespoons sugar
1/2 teaspoon vanilla extract

Shortcakes and Assembly
1 2/3 cups all-purpose flour
2 tablespoons sugar
1 tablespoon baking powder
3/4 teaspoon salt
1/2 cup (1 stick) unsalted butter, chilled
   and cut into small pieces
3/4 cup buttermilk
1/2 teaspoon vanilla extract
1/4 cup (1/2 stick) butter, melted
1/4 cup sugar

To prepare the topping, toss the raspberries, sugar and orange zest in a bowl. Chill, covered, until serving time.

To prepare the whipped cream, beat the cream, sugar and vanilla in a mixing bowl at medium-high speed for 2 minutes or until soft peaks form. Chill, covered, for up to 2 hours.

To prepare the shortcakes, whisk the flour, 2 tablespoons sugar, the baking powder and salt in a bowl until combined. Using a pastry blender, cut in 1/2 cup butter until the mixture is the consistency of coarse meal. Add the buttermilk and vanilla and toss with a fork or a rubber spatula just until moistened and blended.

Gently press the dough into a thick 4×6-inch rectangle on a lightly floured surface. Trim the edges even and cut the rectangle into six equal squares. Arrange the squares well apart on an ungreased baking sheet. Brush with 1/4 cup melted butter and sprinkle with 1/4 cup sugar. Bake at 400 degrees for 15 to 18 minutes or until the shortcakes are puffed and golden brown. Remove to a wire rack to cool slightly or completely.

Split the shortcakes horizontally into halves and arrange the bottom halves cut sides up on each of six dessert plates. Spoon equal portions of the raspberries over each half. Layer with a dollop of whipped cream and the remaining shortcake tops cut sides down. Serve immediately.
Serves 6

This recipe is excellent using any fresh fruit. Mix blueberries and raspberries for a special Fourth of July version.

Photograph for this recipe is shown on page 133.

Carrot Cake with Cream Cheese Frosting

Cake
2 cups all-purpose flour
2 teaspoons baking soda
2 teaspoons ground cinnamon
1/2 teaspoon salt
2 cups sugar
3/4 cup buttermilk
3/4 cup vegetable oil
3 eggs
2 teaspoons vanilla extract
2 cups grated carrots

1 cup chopped pecans
1 (8-ounce) can crushed pineapple,
   drained
1 (3-ounce) can flaked coconut

Cream Cheese Frosting
11 ounces cream cheese, softened
3/4 cup (1 1/2 sticks) butter or
   margarine, softened
3 cups sifted confectioners' sugar
1 1/2 teaspoons vanilla extract

To prepare the cake, sift the flour, baking soda, cinnamon and salt together. Combine the sugar, buttermilk, oil, eggs and vanilla in a mixing bowl and beat at medium speed until blended. Reduce the speed to low and add the flour mixture, carrots, pecans, pineapple and coconut. Beat until combined.

Spoon the batter evenly into three 9-inch cake pans sprayed with nonstick cooking spray. Bake at 350 degrees for 25 to 30 minutes or until wooden picks inserted in the centers come out clean. Cool in the pans for 5 minutes. Invert onto a wire rack to cool completely.

To prepare the frosting, beat the cream cheese and butter in a mixing bowl at medium speed until creamy. Add the confectioners' sugar and vanilla and beat until smooth and fluffy. Spread the frosting between the layers and over the side and top of the cake.
Makes 1 (9-inch) 3-layer cake

This recipe can easily be used to make a sheet cake or cupcakes.

Gingerbread Cake

1 cup all-purpose flour
1 tablespoon ground ginger
$1/2$ teaspoon baking soda
$1/8$ teaspoon salt
$1/2$ teaspoon pumpkin pie spice
$1/2$ cup sugar
$1/4$ cup applesauce
2 tablespoons unsalted butter, softened
2 tablespoons molasses
$1/2$ cup buttermilk
1 egg

Mix the flour, ginger, baking soda, salt and pumpkin pie spice together. Beat the sugar, applesauce, butter and molasses in a mixing bowl at medium speed until blended. Alternately add the dry ingredients and buttermilk to the applesauce mixture, beginning and ending with the flour and beating at low speed until blended after each addition. Add the egg and beat at medium speed for 1 minute.

Spoon the batter into a 5×9-inch loaf pan sprayed with nonstick cooking spray. Bake at 350 degrees for 55 to 60 minutes or until a wooden pick inserted in the center comes out clean. Cool in the pan for 5 to 10 minutes and remove to a wire rack to cool completely.

Serves 6

Chocolate Fudge

4 ounces unsweetened chocolate
1 (1-pound) package confectioners' sugar, sifted
1/8 teaspoon salt
6 ounces cream cheese, softened
1/2 teaspoon vanilla extract
1 cup chopped pecans

Line the bottom of an 8×8-inch dish with waxed paper. Microwave the chocolate in a microwave-safe dish until melted, stirring frequently. Mix the confectioners' sugar and salt in a bowl.

Beat the cream cheese in a mixing bowl of an electric mixer fitted with a whisk attachment until creamy. Gradually add the confectioners' sugar mixture to the cream cheese, beating constantly until smooth. Blend in the vanilla. Add the chocolate and beat until smooth, scraping the side of the bowl with a rubber spatula as needed. Fold in the pecans.

Press the chocolate mixture into the prepared dish. Chill for 2 hours or until firm. Cut into 1-inch squares.

Makes 64 squares

Cranberry-Orange Chocolate Truffles

4 cups confectioners' sugar, sifted
8 ounces cream cheese, softened
2 cups dried cranberries
Grated zest of 3 oranges
5 ounces unsweetened chocolate, melted
1 teaspoon vanilla extract
1 cup baking cocoa

Process the confectioners' sugar, cream cheese, cranberries and orange zest in a food processor until combined. Add the chocolate and vanilla and process until combined. Pour the truffle mixture into a bowl and chill for 1 hour or until firm enough to handle.

Using a small melon baller, shape the truffle mixture into balls. Roll each in the baking cocoa. Arrange the truffles in a single layer on a baking sheet and chill until ready to serve.

Makes 40 truffles

Gingersnaps

2 cups all-purpose flour
2 teaspoons baking soda
2 teaspoons ground ginger
1 teaspoon ground cinnamon
1/2 teaspoon ground cloves
1/2 teaspoon salt
Pinch of nutmeg
3/4 cup (1 1/2 sticks) unsalted
    butter, softened

1 cup sugar
1 egg
1 teaspoon vanilla extract
1/4 cup molasses
Sugar for coating

Whisk the flour, baking soda, ginger, cinnamon, cloves, salt and nutmeg in a bowl until combined. Beat the butter and 1 cup sugar in a mixing bowl at medium speed for 3 minutes or until creamy. Add the egg and vanilla and beat until blended. Gradually add the flour mixture, beating constantly at low speed until smooth, scraping the side of the bowl as needed. Fold in the molasses.

Shape the dough into 1-inch balls and then coat with sugar. Arrange the balls 3 inches apart on a cookie sheet sprayed with nonstick cooking spray. Bake at 350 degrees for 15 to 20 minutes or until the cookies spread and the surfaces are cracked. Cool on the cookie sheet for 2 minutes and remove to a wire rack to cool completely. Store in an airtight container.

Makes about 40 cookies

Almond Spice Cookies

Cookies
1 cup whole unblanched almonds
2/3 cup sugar
4 cups all-purpose flour
1 tablespoon baking cocoa
2 teaspoons ground cinnamon
2 teaspoons baking powder
1 teaspoon ground cloves
Pinch of ground nutmeg
Grated zest of 1 orange
1/2 cup (1 stick) unsalted butter, chilled
    and cut into small pieces

4 eggs
1/3 cup sweet white wine
1 teaspoon vanilla extract

Confectioners' Sugar Glaze
1 (1-pound) package confectioners'
    sugar
1/2 cup orange juice
3 tablespoons water

To prepare the cookies, process the almonds and sugar in a food processor until the almonds are finely ground. Add the flour, baking cocoa, cinnamon, baking powder, cloves, nutmeg and orange zest and pulse just until combined. Add the butter and pulse several times until the mixture is the consistency of coarse meal.

Place the flour mixture in a mixing bowl of an electric mixer fitted with a whisk attachment. Add the eggs one at a time, beating at medium-low speed until combined after each addition. Add the wine and vanilla and beat until blended.

Shape the dough by tablespoonfuls into balls and arrange on a cookie sheet lined with baking parchment. Gently press the balls into discs and bake at 375 degrees for 10 to 12 minutes or until golden brown. Cool on the cookie sheet and then remove to a wire rack. Place the wire rack over a baking sheet.

To prepare the glaze, sift the confectioners' sugar into a mixing bowl and add the orange juice and water. Whisk until smooth and of a glaze consistency. Coat the cookies with the glaze. Gently run a flat metal spatula under the cookies while the glaze is drying to prevent the cookies from sticking to the rack.

Makes about 5 dozen cookies

Store in an airtight container for up to one week. These cookies characteristically have a drier consistency, so enjoy dipping them in tea or coffee.

Harvest Cookies

1 1/2 cups all-purpose flour
1 teaspoon baking soda
1 teaspoon ground cinnamon
1/2 teaspoon ground cloves
1/4 teaspoon salt
Pinch of nutmeg
1 cup (2 sticks) unsalted
   butter, softened
1 cup packed light brown sugar
3/4 cup granulated sugar

1 egg
2 teaspoons vanilla extract
3 cups quick-cooking oats
1 cup walnuts, chopped
1/2 cup dried cranberries
1/2 cup golden raisins
1/2 cup dried peach, finely chopped
1/2 cup dried apple, finely chopped
Granulated sugar for coating

Whisk the flour, baking soda, cinnamon, cloves, salt and nutmeg in a bowl until combined. Beat the butter, brown sugar and 3/4 cup granulated sugar in a mixing bowl at medium-high speed for 3 minutes or until light and fluffy. Add the egg and beat until blended. Beat in the vanilla. Add the flour mixture and beat just until combined. Mix in the oats, walnuts, cranberries, raisins, peach and apple.

Shape the dough by tablespoonfuls into balls and arrange on a wax paper-lined cookie sheet. Dip the base of a flat cup in granulated sugar and press the balls into small discs. Bake at 350 degrees for 10 to 12 minutes or until golden brown. Cool on the cookie sheet for 2 minutes. Remove to a wire rack to cool completely. Store in an airtight container.

Makes about 40 cookies

Pumpkin Pie

2 1/2 cups canned pumpkin purée
8 ounces cream cheese, softened
3 eggs, lightly beaten
1/4 cup packed brown sugar
1 teaspoon ground cinnamon
1/2 teaspoon salt

1/2 teaspoon ground ginger
1/2 teaspoon freshly grated nutmeg
1/4 teaspoon each ground mace, ground
   allspice and ground cloves
1 cup sweetened condensed milk
1 (9-inch) deep-dish pie shell

Whisk the pumpkin and cream cheese in a bowl until smooth. Add the eggs, brown sugar, cinnamon, salt, ginger, nutmeg, mace, allspice and cloves and whisk until combined. Whisk in the condensed milk.

Spoon the pumpkin mixture into the pie shell and bake at 350 degrees for 45 minutes or until the center is set. Cool on a wire rack until room temperature and then chill until serving time. Garnish each serving with a dollop of whipped cream.

Serves 8

Entertainment

Turtle Brownies

Blonde Brownies

Espresso Brownies

Chocolate Brownie Icing

Chocolate Chip Walnut Cookies

Seven-Layer Bars

Chocolate Marshmallows

Fresh Lemon Bars

Lemon-Lavender Tea Cakes

Sausage Balls

Football Chicken Wings

Marinated Shrimp

Parmesan-Coconut Fried Shrimp

Smoked Trout, Tarragon and Tomato Tarts

Phyllo Tarts with Dates and Goat Cheese

Cranberry-Brie Tarts

Cranberry Relish

Artichoke-Stuffed Mushrooms

Smoked Salmon Tea Sandwiches

Cucumber-Dill Tea Sandwiches

Vine-Ripened Tomato Tea Sandwiches

Yellow Tomato Bruschetta

Blue Cheese, Walnut and Raspberry Jewels

Blue Cheese Deviled Eggs

Cheese Platter

Honey-Lavender Spice Butter

Warm Artichoke Dip

Dill and Artichoke Hummus

White Bean and Ham Dip

Mango Chutney

Buttermilk Ranch Dressing

Blue Cheese Dressing

Marshmallow Dip

Curried Pumpkin Seeds

Spiced Pecans

Strawberry Orange Floats

Summer Punch

Raspberry Lemonade

Limeade with Mint

Peach Iced Tea

Chai Tea

After-Dinner Coffee

Entertaining with the Café

Larry D. Morrell

Larry's life after high school seemed normal enough. He was a student at Savannah Technical College and worked at the Savannah College of Art and Design. Then he started doing all of the wrong things. He partied with his friends, which became more important to him than anything else. He dropped out of school. He quit his job. He got lazy.

"It was all my fault," he says now with a smile, "Partying all of the time—it was all that I cared about."

Then his cousin told him about an accelerated culinary arts program that was affiliated with Savannah Tech, and Larry saw his opportunity to start over. He immediately enrolled at the Starfish Café. He was excited to be back in the classroom. His family grew hopeful that he would stick to it this time.

Larry excelled and was selected as student of the week. Any negativity in his life seemed to evaporate.

"Chef Rachel and Chef Bob really wanted me to get the big picture. It wasn't just about culinary arts. It was about life. They wanted me to be successful. It helped me to change."

At graduation, Larry was chosen by the class to be the speaker.

"That day I felt so good. Afterwards, when we walked outside, I saw a rainbow in the sky and knew that I could do anything. Since then, I've done everything that I've wanted to do."

Larry has been a part of the Chef team at Elizabeth on 37th since then, and he feels an incredible sense of accomplishment being part of one of Savannah's most famous eateries. "Everyone there is so good at what they do that I had to step it up," he now says with pride. "They are my new friends. They pitched in and helped me learn the things that I needed to succeed."

Now Larry's life is a good one. He has his own place. He loves his work and has been at Elizabeth on 37th for over two years. When asked about the people that he used to party with, Larry smiles and says, "I don't have anything in common with them anymore. Now it's all about the future."

Stephen Borros III

Homelessness can happen to anybody, just ask Stephen. He had recently relocated to Savannah, found an apartment, and obtained a job as an administrative assistant. Within two weeks the job was eliminated. A few weeks later he lost his apartment. He was suddenly homeless and sleeping on the streets.

"It was not why I moved here," he explains with a shrug. "You never think it'll happen to you, but oh boy!"

Sitting in one of Savannah's many squares one day, Stephen was trying to figure out what to do. "I was sitting on the bench when this guy sits down and starts talking to me. We talked about the weather and I guess that I looked a little rugged. He asked me if I was ok and I told him that I was, but he kept on asking questions. He said that he knew of this place that got people back on their feet. He asked me if I had any cooking experience and then we walked to the Starfish Café."

Stephen was introduced to Chef Rachel and the Employment & Training Center staff. Two days later he started class.

"I used my stipend to get a room. Fifty dollars is a lot of money when you don't have any," he smiles.

"It's not easy being here," Stephen says, "but hard work, being fair, and using the support system that is given to you is the key. Then you find that there is a golden nugget at the end."

Chef Lo helped Stephen get a job at the Bonna Bella Yacht Club, so in addition to being a full-time student, he suddenly had a full-time job too.

He graduated and was hired as the Chef at the Savannah Tea Room, and the future was suddenly very bright.

"It teaches you a lot," he concludes of the experience. "It teaches you to save a little more and plan a little better, but I feel good about the opportunities that I now have because of this place."

Turtle Brownies

2 1/4 cups all-purpose flour, sifted
2 1/2 cups sugar
1 teaspoon salt
1 1/2 cups (3 sticks) unsalted butter, softened
3 cups (18 ounces) chocolate chips
6 eggs, at room temperature
1 tablespoon vanilla extract
1 1/2 cups walnuts, chopped
1 jar caramel sauce

Lightly butter and flour a 9×13-inch baking dish and line the bottom with waxed paper. Mix the flour, sugar and salt with a fork in a bowl. Place the butter and chocolate chips in a microwave-safe bowl. Microwave on High at 30-second intervals until melted, stirring after each interval. Whisk in the eggs one at a time. Stir in the flour mixture and vanilla. Fold in the walnuts. Pour into the prepared baking dish and spread evenly. Bake at 350 degrees for 30 to 45 minutes or until a wooden pick inserted in the center comes out almost completely clean. Cool completely in the pan on a wire rack

To serve, cut into squares and place on a dessert plate. Drizzle with the caramel sauce.

Makes one 9×13-inch dish

Photograph for this recipe is shown on page 167.

Blonde Brownies

2 cups packed brown sugar
1²/3 cups unsalted butter
2¹/2 cups all-purpose flour
1 tablespoon baking powder
1 teaspoon salt
3 eggs
5 tablespoons bourbon
1 tablespoon vanilla extract
1²/3 cups chopped pecans, toasted
16 ounces white chocolate chips

Line a 9×13-inch baking pan with baking parchment. Heat the brown sugar and butter in a saucepan over medium heat until melted, stirring frequently. Bring the mixture to a full boil and boil for 1 minute. Remove from the heat and cool completely. (You may chill in the refrigerator to speed up the process.)

Sift the flour, baking powder and salt together. Spoon the cooled brown sugar mixture into a mixing bowl. Whisk in the eggs one at a time at medium speed, scraping down the side of the bowl after each addition. Add the bourbon and vanilla and mix well. Add the flour mixture and mix well. Stir in the pecans and white chocolate chips. Pour into the prepared pan. Bake at 350 degrees for 30 to 40 minutes or until a wooden pick inserted in the center comes out clean. Remove from the oven and cool completely before cutting into squares.

Makes one 9×13-inch pan

Espresso Brownies

1 cup (2 sticks) unsalted butter
1/2 cup unsweetened baking chocolate
1 cup (6 ounces) semisweet
    chocolate chips
2 1/2 cups sugar
2 teaspoons vanilla extract

4 eggs
2 cups all-purpose flour
1 teaspoon baking powder
1/2 teaspoon salt
2 tablespoons instant espresso powder
4 teaspoons hot water

Grease a 9×13-inch baking pan with additional butter or nonstick cooking spray. Place 1 cup butter, the unsweetened baking chocolate and chocolate chips in a medium microwave-safe bowl. Microwave on High at 1-minute intervals until melted and smooth, stirring after each interval. Stir in the sugar and vanilla. Add the eggs one at a time, mixing well after each addition. Add the flour, baking powder and salt and mix just until all the ingredients are moistened and smooth. Dissolve the espresso powder in the hot water in a bowl. Stir into the batter. Spread the batter in the prepared pan. Bake at 350 degrees for 30 to 40 minutes or until the brownies just begin to pull away from the sides of the pan. Do not overbake. Remove from the oven and cool completely. Cut into large bars.

Makes 12 large brownies

Chocolate Brownie Icing

1 cup (6 ounces) chocolate chips
1/4 cup (1/2 stick) unsalted butter
2 tablespoons corn syrup

Place the chocolate chips and butter in a microwave-safe bowl. Microwave on High at 30-second intervals until the chocolate is melted, stirring after each interval. Stir in the corn syrup. To use, spread the icing over any of our cooled brownies.

Makes 1 1/2 cups

Chocolate Chip Walnut Cookies

1¹/4 cups all-purpose flour
¹/2 teaspoon salt
¹/2 teaspoon baking soda
¹/2 cup (1 stick) unsalted butter, softened
¹/2 cup packed light brown sugar
¹/2 cup granulated sugar
1 egg
1 teaspoon vanilla extract
2 cups (12 ounces) chocolate chips
³/4 cup coarsely chopped walnuts

Spray two cookie sheets with nonstick cooking spray. Whisk the flour, salt and baking soda in a bowl. Beat the butter, brown sugar and granulated sugar at medium speed in a mixing bowl for 3 minutes or until light and fluffy. Add the egg and vanilla and mix well. Add the flour mixture and beat at low speed until combined, scraping down the side of the bowl with a rubber spatula. Fold in the chocolate chips and walnuts. Drop by tablespoonfuls 3 inches apart on the prepared cookie sheets. Bake for 12 to 15 minutes or until golden brown. Cool on a wire rack.

Makes about 30 cookies

Seven-Layer Bars

1/4 cup (1/2 stick) unsalted butter, melted
1 1/2 cups graham cracker crumbs
Pinch of salt
1 cup sweetened condensed milk
1 cup (6 ounces) semisweet chocolate chips
1 cup flaked coconut
1 cup pecan pieces
1 cup (6 ounces) butterscotch chips

Mix the butter, graham cracker crumbs and salt in a small bowl. Press into a greased 5×8-inch baking pan. Pour the condensed milk over the graham cracker mixture. Layer the chocolate chips, flaked coconut, pecan pieces and butterscotch chips over the condensed milk layer in the order listed. Bake at 325 degrees for 30 minutes. Remove from the oven to cool. Cut into bars.

Makes 1 dozen bars

Chocolate Marshmallows

1 envelope unflavored gelatin
1/4 cup water
1/3 cup corn syrup
1/2 cup sifted baking cocoa
3/4 cup sugar
1/8 teaspoon salt
1/4 cup water
1/2 teaspoon vanilla extract

Spray a 9×13-inch pan with nonstick cooking spray and line the bottom with waxed paper. Soften the gelatin in 1/4 cup water in a mixing bowl for 6 minutes. Bring the corn syrup, baking cocoa, sugar, salt and 1/4 cup water to a boil in a medium saucepan. Boil for 3 minutes and remove from the heat. Beat the softened gelatin at low speed until well mixed. Add the baking cocoa mixture gradually, beating constantly. Gradually increase the speed to high and beat for 10 minutes or until the mixture is thick, creamy and tripled in volume. Beat in the vanilla. Pour into the prepared pan. Let stand, uncovered, at room temperature for 8 hours or until firm. Cut the marshmallows into cubes. Store in an airtight container for up to 2 weeks.
Makes 40 marshmallows

To make Vanilla Marshmallows, omit the baking cocoa and increase the vanilla to 1 tablespoon.

Fresh Lemon Bars

2 cups all-purpose flour
1/2 cup confectioners' sugar
1 cup (2 sticks) butter or margarine, softened
1/4 cup all-purpose flour
1/2 teaspoon baking powder
4 eggs
2 cups granulated sugar
1/3 cup fresh lemon juice
Zest of 3 lemons
Confectioners' sugar for sprinkling

Butter and flour a 9×13-inch baking pan. Line the bottom of the pan with waxed paper. Pulse 2 cups flour and 1/2 cup confectioners' sugar in a food processor until well combined. Add the butter and pulse until the mixture resembles coarse cornmeal. Press the dough firmly into the prepared baking pan. Bake at 350 degrees for 20 to 25 minutes or until light brown. Remove from the oven to cool. Maintain the oven temperature.

Mix 1/4 cup flour and the baking powder together. Whisk the eggs in a large bowl. Whisk in the granulated sugar, lemon juice and lemon zest. Whisk in the flour mixture. Pour over the cooled crust. Bake for 25 minutes or until set. Remove to a wire rack to cool completely. Cut into bars and sprinkle with confectioners' sugar.
Makes one 9×13-inch pan

Lemon-Lavender Tea Cakes

2^{1}/$_{2}$ cups all-purpose flour
2 teaspoons baking powder
Pinch of salt
^{1}/$_{2}$ cup (1 stick) unsalted butter, softened
1 cup sugar
2 eggs
1 teaspoon lemon extract
Zest of 1 lemon
1 tablespoon dried lavender
^{1}/$_{4}$ cup heavy cream
^{1}/$_{3}$ cup sugar

Mix the flour, baking powder and salt together. Beat the butter and 1 cup sugar in a mixing bowl for 4 minutes or until light and fluffy. Add the eggs one at a time, beating well after each addition. Beat in the lemon extract, lemon zest and lavender. Add the flour mixture and cream alternately one-half at a time, beating constantly at medium-low speed. Cover and chill the dough for 1 to 24 hours.

Remove the dough from the refrigerator. Shape the dough by tablespoonfuls into balls. Roll the balls in ^{1}/$_{3}$ cup sugar and place on an ungreased baking sheet. Gently press the balls into discs. Bake at 375 degrees for 15 minutes or until golden brown. Remove from the oven and cool on the cookie sheet for 5 minutes before serving.
Makes about 2 dozen

These cookies will last for up to a week stored in an airtight container.

Sausage Balls

3 cups all-purpose baking mix
1 pound ground hot pork sausage
2 cups (8 ounces) shredded sharp Cheddar cheese

Combine the baking mix, sausage and cheese in a large bowl and mix together with your hands. Shape into 3/4-inch balls and place on lightly greased baking sheets. Bake at 400 degrees for 15 to 18 minutes or until light brown.
Serves a crowd

Football Chicken Wings

3 cups all-purpose flour
2 tablespoons garlic powder
2 tablespoons onion powder
1 teaspoon cayenne pepper
1 teaspoon ground ginger
3 pounds chicken wings

Salt and black pepper to taste
Vegetable oil for frying
1/2 cup hot sauce
1/2 cup (1 stick) unsalted butter, melted
1/4 cup apple cider vinegar

Mix the flour, garlic powder, onion powder, cayenne pepper and ginger in a large sealable freezer bag. Season the chicken wings with salt and black pepper. Add the chicken wings to the flour mixture in batches and shake until coated. Fry the chicken wings in batches in hot oil in a deep fryer or deep skillet over medium-high heat for 8 minutes or until cooked through and crispy. Drain on paper towels and keep warm until all of the chicken wings are cooked.

Whisk the hot sauce, butter and vinegar in a medium bowl. Toss the chicken wings in the sauce or serve with the sauce on the side. Serve the chicken wings with Buttermilk Ranch Dressing (page 195), Blue Cheese Dressing (page 195), celery sticks and carrot sticks.
Serves 4 to 6

Marinated Shrimp

1 cup olive oil
3/4 cup red wine vinegar
1 teaspoon celery seeds
1 tablespoon horseradish
1 tablespoon mustard seeds
1 tablespoon coriander
2 tablespoons lemon juice
1 teaspoon minced garlic
1/2 teaspoon salt
Pinch of pepper
1 teaspoon sugar
1/2 teaspoon Tabasco sauce
2 pounds cooked medium shrimp,
    peeled and deveined
1 purple onion, thinly sliced
1/4 cup capers
2 red tomatoes, seeded and chopped

Whisk the olive oil, vinegar, celery seeds, horseradish, mustard seeds, coriander, lemon juice, garlic, salt, pepper, sugar and Tabasco sauce in a medium bowl. Combine the shrimp, onion, capers and tomatoes in a large bowl and toss to mix. Pour the marinade over the shrimp mixture. Marinate, covered, in the refrigerator for 24 hours before serving.
Serves 6 to 8

These shrimp are great alone or served on toast rounds. Be sure to eat them with the onion, capers and tomatoes.

Parmesan-Coconut Fried Shrimp

1 pound unpeeled fresh medium shrimp
1 1/2 cups all-purpose flour
1 teaspoon salt
1/2 teaspoon pepper
1/4 cup heavy cream
2 eggs, lightly beaten
1 cup (4 ounces) shredded Parmesan cheese
2 cups flaked coconut
Vegetable oil for frying

Peel and devein the shrimp, leaving the tails intact. Mix the flour, salt and pepper in a medium bowl. Blend the cream and eggs in a bowl. Mix the Parmesan cheese and coconut in a bowl. Coat each shrimp with the flour mixture, then dip in the egg mixture. Roll in the coconut mixture to coat. Fry in batches in hot oil in a deep saucepan over high heat until golden brown and cooked through. Drain on paper towels. Serve immediately with sweet-and-sour sauce.

Serves 4 to 6

Smoked Trout, Tarragon and Tomato Tarts

1 cup chopped smoked trout
2 tablespoons minced sun-dried tomatoes
1 teaspoon minced fresh tarragon
1 cup finely chopped buffalo mozzarella cheese
1 (15-count) package miniature phyllo shells

Combine the trout, sun-dried tomatoes, tarragon and cheese in a small bowl and toss to mix. Fill each phyllo shell full with the trout mixture and arrange on a baking sheet. Bake at 375 degrees for 7 minutes or until heated through.
Makes 15

Phyllo Tarts with Dates and Goat Cheese

1/2 cup dried dates, chopped
2 tablespoons brown sugar
1 cup crumbled goat cheese
Pinch of ground cinnamon
1 (15-count) package miniature phyllo shells

Combine the dates, brown sugar, goat cheese and cinnamon in a small bowl and mix well. Fill each phyllo shell full with the date mixture and arrange on a baking sheet. Bake at 375 degrees for 7 minutes or until heated through.
Makes 15

Cranberry-Brie Tarts

1 small round Brie cheese, rind removed
1 cup Cranberry Relish (below)
1 (15-count) package miniature phyllo shells

Finely chop the cheese. Fill each phyllo shell one-half full with the cheese. Top each with a dollop of the Cranberry Relish and arrange on a baking sheet. Bake for 7 minutes or until heated through.
Makes 15

Cranberry Relish

Juice and zest of 1 orange
2 cups dried cranberries
2 cups water
1 cup sugar

Combine the orange juice, orange zest, cranberries, water and sugar in a small saucepan and mix well. Bring to a boil and reduce the heat. Simmer for 5 minutes. Remove from the heat to cool. Store in an airtight container in the refrigerator for up to 2 weeks.
Makes 4 to 5 cups

This relish is great spread on sandwiches, served with pork, and spread on warm biscuits.

Artichoke-Stuffed Mushrooms

1 pound large mushrooms
1 tablespoon olive oil
1/4 cup chopped yellow onion
2 garlic cloves, chopped
1/4 cup pesto
1/4 cup panko
1 (14-ounce) can artichoke hearts,
    drained and chopped
1/4 cup sun-dried tomatoes, chopped
4 ounces cream cheese,
    cut into cubes and softened
Salt and pepper to taste
1/2 cup (2 ounces) grated Parmesan cheese
1/4 cup fresh Italian parsley, chopped

Remove the stems from the mushrooms and discard. Lightly rinse the mushrooms
and pat dry with paper towels. Heat the olive oil in a medium sauté pan over
medium-high heat. Add the onion and sauté for 2 minutes. Add the garlic and sauté
for 1 minute. Remove from the heat and spoon into a medium bowl. Add the pesto,
bread crumbs, artichoke hearts, sun-dried tomatoes and cream cheese and stir to mix.
Season with salt and pepper. Fill each mushroom cap heaping full with the artichoke
mixture and sprinkle with the Parmesan cheese. Place the stuffed mushrooms on a
baking sheet. Bake at 350 degrees for 15 minutes or until the filling is hot and the
cheese melts. Arrange the stuffed mushrooms on a platter and sprinkle with the parsley.
Serves 12

Smoked Salmon Tea Sandwiches

1/4 cup (1/2 stick) unsalted butter, softened
2 ounces cream cheese, softened
1 tablespoon capers, minced
1 tablespoon chopped fresh parsley
1 tablespoon minced purple onion
Pinch of salt and pepper
8 thin slices wheat sandwich bread, crusts trimmed
8 thin slices smoked salmon

Whisk the butter, cream cheese, capers, parsley, onion, salt and pepper in a mixing
bowl until creamy. Spread the cream cheese mixture evenly on one side of each slice
of bread. Layer the salmon evenly over the cream cheese side of one-half of the bread
slices. Place the remaining bread slices cream cheese side down over the salmon.
Cut each sandwich into quarters and serve.
Makes 16 tea sandwiches

Cucumber-Dill Tea Sandwiches

1/4 cup (1/2 stick) unsalted butter, softened
2 ounces cream cheese, softened
1 tablespoon chopped fresh dill weed
Pinch of salt and pepper
8 thin slices white sandwich bread, crusts trimmed
24 thin slices cucumber

Whisk the butter, cream cheese, dill weed, salt and pepper in a mixing bowl until creamy. Spread the cream cheese mixture evenly on one side of each slice of bread. Layer the cucumber slices evenly on the cream cheese side of one-half of the bread slices. Place the remaining bread slices cream cheese side down over the cucumber slices. Cut each sandwich into quarters and serve.

Makes 16 tea sandwiches

Vine-Ripened Tomato Tea Sandwiches

1/4 cup (1/2 stick) unsalted butter, softened
2 ounces cream cheese, softened
1 tablespoon chopped fresh parsley
Pinch of salt and pepper
8 thin slices white sandwich bread, crusts trimmed
16 thin slices vine-ripened tomatoes

Whisk the butter, cream cheese, parsley, salt and pepper in a mixing bowl until creamy. Spread the cream cheese mixture evenly on one side of each slice of the bread. Layer the tomato slices evenly on the cream cheese side of one-half of the bread slices. Place the remaining bread slices cream cheese side down over the tomato slices. Cut each sandwich into quarters and serve.

Makes 16 tea sandwiches

Yellow Tomato Bruschetta

4 vine-ripened yellow tomatoes,
    finely chopped
1/4 cup chopped fresh basil
1 teaspoon minced garlic
1 shallot, minced
1/4 cup olive oil
1 1/2 cups (6 ounces) finely chopped fresh
    mozzarella cheese
Salt and pepper to taste
1 French baguette

Combine the tomatoes, basil, garlic, shallot, olive oil and mozzarella cheese in a medium bowl and toss to mix. Season with salt and pepper. Cut the baguette crosswise into slices 1/4 inch thick. Top each baguette slice with a heaping portion of the tomato mixture and place on a baking sheet. Broil until the mozzarella cheese is bubbly and golden brown.

Serves 6 to 8

Blue Cheese, Walnut and Raspberry Jewels

8 ounces crumbled blue cheese
1/2 cup (1 stick) butter, softened
1 1/3 cups all-purpose flour
Pinch of salt
Pinch of pepper
3 tablespoons finely ground walnuts
1/3 cup raspberry preserves

Beat the blue cheese and butter at medium speed in a mixing bowl until blended. Add the flour, salt, pepper and walnuts and mix until combined. Shape into 1-inch balls and arrange 2 inches apart on a greased baking sheet. Chill, covered, for 1 hour. Remove from the refrigerator and press an indention with your thumb in the center of each ball. Fill each indentation with a dollop of the raspberry preserves. Bake at 325 degrees for 15 minutes. Remove from the oven and cool before serving.
Makes 3 dozen

Blue Cheese Deviled Eggs

1 dozen eggs
2 tablespoons white vinegar
5 slices bacon, cooked and crumbled
1/2 cup crumbled blue cheese
1/4 cup mayonnaise
2 tablespoons finely ground pecans
1/4 teaspoon salt
11/2 teaspoons freshly ground pepper

Place the eggs in a large saucepan and add enough water to cover. Add the vinegar.
Bring to a boil over high heat. Boil for 7 minutes. Remove from the heat and let
stand for 2 minutes. Cool the eggs and peel. Cut the eggs into halves lengthwise.
Carefully remove the yolks and place in a bowl, reserving the egg whites. Mash the
egg yolks until smooth. Add the bacon, blue cheese, mayonnaise, pecans, salt and pepper
and mix well. Spoon the egg yolk mixture evenly into the reserved egg whites.
Makes 2 dozen

*The vinegar is added to the cooking water to help keep the egg shells from sticking to
the egg while peeling. Also, for special occasions spoon the egg yolk mixture into a pastry
bag fitted with the desired tip and pipe into the egg whites. Garnish with finely chopped
fresh chives.*

Cheese Platter

1/4 cup apple cider vinegar
1/4 teaspoon salt
2 tablespoons minced pimentos
1 teaspoon minced pickled jalapeño chile
2 tablespoons olive oil
1 teaspoon minced fresh chives
1 small round Brie cheese
1 medium wedge Stilton cheese
1 cup fresh raspberries
1/4 cup Spiced Pecans, chopped (page 197)
8 (1/2-inch-thick) slices sharp Cheddar cheese
8 (1/2-inch-thick) slices cream cheese

Combine the vinegar, salt, pimentos, jalapeño chile, olive oil and chives in a small
bowl and mix well. Place the Brie cheese and Stilton cheese on opposite ends of a
serving platter. Top the Brie cheese with the raspberries and the Stilton cheese with
the Spiced Pecans. Alternate the Cheddar cheese and cream cheese slices slightly
overlapping in the center of the platter. Pour the pimento mixture over the Cheddar
cheese and cream cheese. Serve with thin black pepper crackers.

Serves 4 to 6

Honey-Lavender Spice Butter

1 pound (4 sticks) unsalted butter, softened
1/4 cup honey
1 tablespoon minced lavender
Pinch of salt
Pinch of ground allspice
Pinch of ground cinnamon

Combine the butter, honey, lavender, salt, allspice and cinnamon in a mixing bowl and beat until combined. Use the butter to spread on dinner rolls, breakfast breads or French loaves.
Makes 2 cups

Warm Artichoke Dip

2 (14-ounce) cans artichoke hearts, drained and chopped
1 (10-ounce) package frozen chopped spinach, thawed and drained
2 garlic cloves, minced
2 tablespoons lemon juice
1/2 cup mayonnaise
2 ounces cream cheese, softened
1 envelope vegetable soup mix
1/2 cup fine dry bread crumbs
1 cup (4 ounces) shredded fresh Parmesan cheese
1/4 cup (1 ounce) grated fresh Parmesan cheese

Combine the artichoke hearts, spinach, garlic, lemon juice, mayonnaise, cream
cheese, vegetable soup mix, bread crumbs and shredded Parmesan cheese in
a mixing bowl and mix well. Spoon into a lightly greased 1-quart baking dish.
Sprinkle with the grated Parmesan cheese. Bake at 350 degrees for 30 minutes
or until bubbly. Serve with crackers.
Serves 6

Dill and Artichoke Hummus

2 cups canned chickpeas
1/2 cup canned artichokes
1 tablespoon lemon juice
Zest of 1 lemon
1/2 cup tahini
1/4 cup olive oil
5 garlic cloves, minced
1 teaspoon ground cumin
2 tablespoons chopped fresh dill weed
1/4 cup kalamata olives
1 teaspoon paprika
Pinch of cayenne pepper
Salt and black pepper to taste

Purée the chickpeas, artichokes, lemon juice, lemon zest, tahini, olive oil, garlic, cumin, dill weed, olives, paprika and cayenne pepper in a food processor or blender. Season with salt and black pepper. Serve with pita chips, crackers or fresh vegetables.
Serves 4 to 6

White Bean and Ham Dip

3 cups canned white beans
1/2 cup finely chopped purple onion
1/2 cup canned diced tomatoes
1 1/2 cups finely chopped honey ham
1 tablespoon chopped fresh parsley
1 teaspoon minced garlic
Juice and zest of 1 lemon
1/4 cup olive oil
1/4 cup red wine vinegar
Salt and pepper to taste

Combine the beans, onion, tomatoes, ham, parsley, garlic, lemon juice, lemon zest, olive oil and vinegar in a medium bowl and mix well. Season with salt and pepper. Serve with pita chips.
Serves 6 to 8

To prepare Pita Chips, cut pita rounds into wedges and brush with olive oil. Sprinkle with a little paprika and place on a baking sheet. Bake at 425 degrees until golden brown and crisp.

Mango Chutney

2 tablespoons pineapple juice
1 tablespoon cider vinegar
3 tablespoons brown sugar
1 teaspoon curry powder
1 tablespoon olive oil
1/2 teaspoon chile flakes
1/4 cup finely chopped red onion
1 tablespoon minced peeled fresh ginger
1/4 cup finely chopped red bell pepper
1 pound fresh mangos, peeled and chopped
1/4 cup golden raisins
2 tablespoons coarsely chopped macadamia nuts, toasted
Salt and pepper to taste

Combine the pineapple juice, vinegar, brown sugar and curry powder in a medium bowl and mix well. Heat the olive oil in a small saucepan over medium-low heat. Add the chile flakes and onion and cook for 3 minutes. Add the ginger and bell pepper and cook for 3 minutes. Add the mangos and cook for 1 minute. Add the brown sugar mixture and bring just to a boil. Remove from the heat and stir in the raisins and macadamia nuts. Season with salt and pepper. Serve with tortilla chips.

Serves 4 to 6

Buttermilk Ranch Dressing

1 cup sour cream
1 cup mayonnaise
1 cup buttermilk
2 tablespoons dried chives

1 teaspoon minced garlic
1 tablespoon minced fresh parsley
Salt and pepper to taste
Hot red pepper sauce to taste

Whisk the sour cream, mayonnaise, buttermilk, chives, garlic, parsley, salt, pepper and hot sauce in a medium bowl until blended. Chill, covered, for 2 hours or longer before serving.
Makes about 3 cups

The perfect dressing and dip for everything.

Blue Cheese Dressing

1 cup mayonnaise
2 tablespoons minced onion
1 tablespoon minced garlic
1/4 cup chopped fresh parsley
1/2 cup sour cream

1 tablespoon lemon juice
1 tablespoon white vinegar
1/4 cup crumbled blue cheese
Salt and pepper to taste

Combine the mayonnaise, onion, garlic, parsley, sour cream, lemon juice, vinegar and blue cheese in a small mixing bowl and mix well. Season with salt and pepper. Chill, covered, for 1 hour or longer before serving.
Makes 1 pint

Not only great on salads, this dressing is also the perfect dip for chicken fingers, chicken wings, and fresh vegetables.

Marshmallow Dip

8 ounces cream cheese, softened
2 cups marshmallow creme
1/2 cup apricot preserves

Combine the cream cheese and marshmallow creme in a small bowl and mix well.
Stir in the apricot preserves. Serve with fresh fruit for dipping.
Serves 6 to 8

*For entertaining, place the Marshmallow Dip and Fudge Sauce (page 123) on a platter
with fresh fruit. Your guests can help themselves.*

Curried Pumpkin Seeds

5 tablespoons hot curry powder
1 teaspoon salt
3 cups pumpkin seeds
2 tablespoons canola oil

Mix the curry powder and salt in a medium bowl. Toss the pumpkin seeds with the
canola oil in a bowl and spread on a baking sheet. Bake at 325 degrees for 15 minutes.
Remove from the oven. Spoon the pumpkin seeds into the curry powder mixture and
toss to coat.
Serves 4

Spiced Pecans

1¹/2 cups packed light brown sugar
¹/2 cup granulated sugar
6 tablespoons ground cinnamon
¹/4 cup salt
1 teaspoon cayenne pepper
1 teaspoon ground cloves
1 teaspoon ground allspice
5 cups pecan halves
1 cup honey

Mix the brown sugar, granulated sugar, cinnamon, salt, cayenne pepper, cloves and allspice in a medium bowl.

Spread the pecans evenly on a baking sheet and drizzle with the honey. Bake at 350 degrees for 8 to 10 minutes or until the honey begins to bubble. Remove from the oven and cool for 1 to 2 minutes. Carefully remove the pecans with a spatula to the brown sugar mixture and toss until coated. Place the pecans on a clean baking sheet, rubbing to remove any excess brown sugar mixture. Let stand for 1 hour or until the pecans are cool and crisp.

Serves 8 to 10

Spiced Pecans make great gifts bagged and tied with a festive ribbon.

Strawberry Orange Floats

1/2 cup fresh strawberries, cut into quarters
4 large scoops of orange sherbet
1 (750-milliliter) bottle Champagne

Divide the strawberries among four large glasses. Top each with a scoop of the sherbet. Pour enough Champagne into each glass to fill.
Serves 4

To make this float nonalcoholic, simply substitute ginger ale for the Champagne.

Summer Punch

1 quart apple juice
1 quart white grape juice
2 cups pineapple juice
2 cups apricot juice
1 orange, sliced
1/2 cup cherries, cut into halves
2 cups sparkling water
1 peach, pitted and sliced

Combine the apple juice, grape juice, pineapple juice, apricot juice, orange slices and cherries in a large container and stir to blend. Chill, covered, in the refrigerator for 8 to 10 hours. Stir the sparkling water into the fruit juice mixture just before serving. Pour over ice and top with the sliced peach.
Serves 8 to 10

Raspberry Lemonade

3 cups water
3/4 cup sugar
1 1/2 cups lemon juice
1 cup frozen raspberries, thawed and puréed

Bring the water and sugar to a boil in a medium saucepan. Boil until the sugar dissolves, stirring constantly. Remove from the heat to cool. Stir in the lemon juice and raspberries. Strain and serve over ice.
Serves 4

Limeade with Mint

1/2 cup water
1 1/2 cups sugar
1 cup chopped fresh mint
2 teaspoons grated lime zest
1 1/2 cups fresh lime juice
5 cups cold water

Bring 1/2 cup water to a boil in a saucepan. Add the sugar, mint and lime zest. Heat until the sugar dissolves, stirring constantly. Remove from the heat and let stand for 10 minutes. Strain the syrup into a large pitcher, discarding the solids. Stir in the lime juice and 5 cups cold water. Chill, covered, for 8 hours before serving.
Makes 8 cups

Peach Iced Tea

1 1/2 quarts (6 cups) peach nectar
1/2 cup sugar
1/2 gallon unsweetened brewed tea, cooled

Bring the peach nectar and sugar to a boil in a small saucepan. Boil until the sugar dissolves, stirring constantly. Remove from the heat to cool. Combine the tea and peach nectar mixture in a pitcher and blend well. Serve over ice and garnish with sprigs of fresh mint.
Serves 8

Chai Tea

1 tablespoon fennel seeds
6 green cardamom pods
12 whole cloves
1 cinnamon stick
1/2 cup grated peeled ginger

6 black peppercorns
7 cups water
2 tablespoons Darjeeling tea leaves
1/4 cup packed brown sugar
3 cups milk

Combine the fennel seeds, cardamom pods, cloves, cinnamon stick, ginger, peppercorns and water in a saucepan. Bring to a boil and boil for 5 minutes. Remove from the heat and steep for 10 minutes. Add the tea. Return to a boil and reduce the heat. Simmer for 5 minutes. Strain the tea, discarding the solids. Return to the saucepan. Stir in the brown sugar and milk. Serve warm.
Serves 4 to 6

This tea may also be served over ice for a refreshing alternative.

After-Dinner Coffee

3 cups brewed coffee
1/2 cup heavy cream
10 squares Andes Crème de Menthe chocolate candies

Combine the coffee, cream and candies in a medium saucepan. Heat until the candies are melted. Pour into coffee cups and serve.
Serves 4 to 6

Any flavor of the Andes chocolates would be wonderful to use in this coffee.

Index

Starfish Café

To order, contact
Union Mission, Inc.
120 Fahm Street
Savannah, GA 31401

Telephone
(912) 236-7423

Fax
(912) 236-3907

Web site
www.unionmission.org

Proceeds benefit the operation of the Starfish Café.